The Drive to 30

YOUR ULTIMATE GUIDE TO SELLING MORE CARS THAN EVER

Chris J. Martinez

J. Joseph Group, LLC

The Drive to 30: Your Ultimate Guide to Selling More Cars than Ever—1st ed.

ISBN 978-0-9979314-3-3

CONTENTS

DISCLAIMER

The information included in this book is for educational purposes only and is not meant to be a substitute for seeking the advice of a professional. The author and publisher have made their best effort to ensure that the information in this book is accurate. However, they make no warranties as to the accuracy or completeness of the contents herein and cannot be held responsible for any errors, omissions or dated material.

This book contains communication strategies, effective suggestions, methods and other advice that, regardless of my own results and experience, may not produce the same results (or any results) for you. The author makes absolutely no guarantee, expressed or implied, that by following the advice you will get the same or any results, as there are many factors and variables in play for any given situation.

By reading this book, you assume all risks associated with using the advice and suggestions provided herein, with a full understanding that you, solely, are responsible for any situation that may occur as a result of putting this information into action in any way and regardless of your interpretation of the advice.

To my wife ,Veronica, for believing in me and for being an amazing mother to my children.

Forward

* * *

Despite the economic crises of previous years, and despite consumers' increasing concerns about spending money, people are still buying cars. In fact, the American automobile industry is thriving. Additionally, with car sales having hit a record high in 2015, the car sales industry is in a historically phenomenal position. In just one year, more than 17 million cars and trucks were sold. It's almost incomprehensible that an industry that was struggling for survival just a few years ago is now in better shape than ever.

This fact is even more surprising given the situation many car dealerships currently find themselves in. As nationwide car sales numbers continue to climb, many dealerships struggle and eventually close. Many dealership owners find themselves falling deeper and deeper into a mess that they themselves created. It seems that no one, save for a select few, is prepared to make the most of the potential for an explosive growth in sales, and the few dealerships that continuing to dominate the market year after year are the ones who most greatly profit. These are the dealerships that truly understand the times we as salespeople find ourselves in and actively take steps to improve their performance to meet the increasing customer demand.

I am grateful to have managed one of those dealerships and this book details the journey of my success into the 30-Car Club.

If you are a floor salesperson, you undoubtedly know how difficult it is to sell a single car. A successful car sale begins with the proper greeting and continues through the demonstration, walk-through, test drive and (hopefully) negotiating table. There are so many points at which something can go wrong, and there are so many changes in direction that can occur within that precious time. Every second counts, and every minute can feel like an eternity. It takes a combination of skill, determination and, sometimes, sheer luck to be successful, and not many salespeople are able to channel that combination.

Selling one car per month is a challenge. Selling ten cars per month is an achievement. Selling 30 cars per month is damn near a miracle. This is why, with few exceptions, salespeople are generally not able to reach that goal. To provide perspective on the challenge, the national daily car sales average for a floor salesperson is eleven cars per month. Through this book, I'm going to teach you how I more than doubled my own sales targets and how you can do the same. While this may sound challenging, I can assure you that with the right action steps, anyone can get there.

As renowned sales trainer Grant Cardone suggests, rather than lower your targets, you need to increase your actions in order to achieve this goal. Increasing your actions is the first requirement of becoming a 30-Car sales professional. You must increase your action with each step by putting greater effort into each endeavor. Simply put, you must become a better salesperson, which requires increased knowledge about how a perfect sales process functions.

Additionally, you'll able to use that increased knowledge to your advantage, at which point you will be far more able to sell thirty cars in a month. This book contains every strategy you need to realize that goal.

To be clear, I didn't aspire to a career in car sales. I never imagined that I would ever set foot on a dealership floor, let alone write books about how to succeed as a salesperson on one. My foray into the world of car sales was a happy accident born of financial necessity. I needed money and, at that point, almost any job would have been fine, but car sales simply happened to be the one that came my way. After joining the car business, I was able to double my income almost instantly. It was fun, I was a natural and, before I knew it, I was consistently selling 30 cars per month.

When I tell the story that way, however, it makes it seem as though it was a piece of cake. It wasn't. Suggesting that selling thirty cars per month is hard is an understatement, given that you are likely beginning at a point where you struggle to sell even ten cars per month. The 30-Car Club likely feels like a distant dream. Rest assured, the issue isn't that you're a weak salesperson; there are all sorts of hurdles standing in the way of you selling thirty cars per month. In this book, I will break down for you how I was able to accomplish my goal as well as the obstacles I faced along the way, along with some of the best ways to solve these problems.

For one thing, in order to sell thirty cars per month, you need to receive at least thirty customers. How many of us can say that we do? Even those of us who do likely cannot sell thirty cars because, regardless of how good of a salesperson you are, it's not possible to have a 100 percent sales record every day.

The bottom line is that if you want to sell thirty cars a month, you need to understand several things:

First, you must know your numbers. Sales is a process of human interaction. Typically, two people negotiate in order to come to a mutually beneficial agreement. That's the human aspect of sales, and it is extremely important to realize its value as a salesperson. However, when looked at from a purely organizational perspective, sales is a numbers game. It's a series of steps specifically shaped to steadily raise those numbers.

Therefore, you have to know the numbers, which means that, as an individual salesperson, you need to know what's required to sell thirty cars per month all by yourself. You need to create a roadmap to get into the 30-Car Club.

When I started off, I was a "regular" car salesman. I had sufficient experience selling new and used vehicles. Later on, I was promoted to General Sales Manager, and I was responsible not just for my own sales performance but also for the performance of my entire team. Being a sales manager added the responsibility of worrying about things that salespeople usually don't need to worry about, but because I wanted to do more, I persisted.

Second, you must work with management to increase walk-in traffic by thinking and acting like a sales manager. Your daily targets depend on how well your sales managers do their jobs, and they require your assistance in their efforts. Therefore, you need to learn how to row two boats at once. Every day I sit with our Internet Director to find ways to bring in traffic through our online efforts, and I work with our Sales Managers and service managers.

Gaining experience with these managerial tasks helped me gain the necessary knowledge and insight into the process as a whole. I was able to utilize this knowledge when I became a sales manager and, therefore, a lot of advice in this book is related to managing the sales process. It doesn't matter if that's not one of your responsibilities. If you're not a good manager, it will be hard for you to sell thirty cars per month. You must appreciate the complexity of the task that lies ahead; not only do you need to sell, you also need to manage.

Third, you must consistently apply your new knowledge and approach. I could have just as easily continued on my path as a sales professional and sold well over thirty cars per month. However, I felt I could be a bigger asset to the company by helping everyone else sell cars as well. Knowing the math can only get you so far. As Grant Cardone said, "Knowledge is power, but only action behind the knowledge is power." You can know all of the information in this book, but without actually applying it, you won't get to the 30-Car Club status. Before you begin on the journey, make sure you thoroughly understand this.

At the end of every meeting, I say to my staff, "If I were to tell you that someone was going to give you $1 million, but the catch was that you had to sell a car that day to get those million dollars, could you figure out a way to sell that car?" In my heart, I believe that everyone would find a way to sell a car. If you can put enough action behind the knowledge you're about to gain, you will surpass the thirty-cars mark many times over.

I am not the best salesman in the world, but what I do have is persistence in learning, studying what it takes and applying what I studied to make it happen. This approach requires constant work and the utmost dedication on your part.

I used to practice my introduction every day. I even used to rehearse the way I greeted clients every single day. I practiced my walk-around every day. I worked on my closing every day. I imagined myself as a prize fighter, putting in the work so that, when I was in front of a customer, my presentation was fluid—no stumbling blocks, no stuttering. If I don't control my thoughts or words, I tend to stutter when speaking quickly. So I practiced and, as a result, achieved my desired results.

Finally, you must get out of obscurity. I asked myself, "If a real estate millionaire like Gary Keller figured out how to market himself, then why wouldn't I market myself in the same way?" That's when I decided to invest money in marketing myself and getting my name everywhere. I sent flyers and became active on social media. I had to increase my powerbase and "get out of obscurity."

Through social media, you have to make sure everyone in your circle knows you're in the car business. Have your friends and family become an extension of your business—your cheerleaders. Through social media, my wife has sold more cars than some of our bottom-level salespeople without even stepping foot through the door of the dealership. It's this circle of contacts that feeds into your output. The hard work you put in cultivating these contacts will be rewarded down the line.

The best of the best realtors market themselves better than most. I applied the same concepts to the car business. I marketed to my current clients for repeat business and referrals and made sure *everyone* knew what I do for a living. I stayed aware of my surroundings and made full use of them. I've sold people coming into our service department for a simple $40 oil change on a $25,000 car. I've bumped into more deals than the salespeople who are simply standing and waiting in the Hope Line because you need to be moving.

Once you're aware of your surroundings, you'll begin to realize that money is everywhere; you only have to pick it up. There are also deals everywhere; you simply have to believe that you're the dealmaker and, as long as you're in front of the customer, you'll make the deal. My mentor always says, "Put the dealmaker in front of the deals," but this only truly worked after hours of practicing and rehearsing my entire presentation. Many salespeople forget that the most important part of their job is actually *selling* the vehicle. Approximately 80 percent of your time should be "selling the features and benefits of the product."

You can't have a "wing it" mentality. That's a surefire way to make bottom-level income selling cars. It's said that you must believe in yourself; I say you must believe in the proven process *until* you can believe in yourself.

I have a beautiful family that drives me every day. I've made more money in the car business than I ever thought possible. This book is not about *what* made me money but how my work ethic, my student mentality and my refusal to settle for the status quo led me to success.

Selling thirty cars per month is extremely rewarding. Doubling your monthly income is just one of the advantages.

Many dealerships offer bonuses for accomplishments such as selling the highest number of cars per month, achieving the highest targets per month, selling the most vehicles of a particular model or hitting the highest sales numbers in a quarter. Along with your monthly commissions and bonuses, you can comfortably make three or even four times what you're making now.

The truth is, however, that nothing—not even the financial incentives—can beat the feeling of being successful at your job. It affects not just your professional endeavors but also your personal life. You're a better person when you're happy (at least I was). I was able to give more time to my family, my wife and my kids. And, since I was happy, I was able to make *them* happy. It's true that money can't buy you happiness, but success sure can. And that, more than money, is what you're seeking when chasing the goal of selling thirty cars per month.

So let's get started!

The Sales Process

* * *

Are you a good salesperson? If so, what makes you good? If not, what stands between you and success? It takes much more than skills or tips and techniques to be a good salesperson. It takes discipline, rigor and a systematic approach to selling that's taken seriously. You need to work hard on it.

Every great salesperson's success story begins with, and ends at, his search for a perfect sales process. The truth is, no one finds it. A perfect process is highly elusive; some would go so far as to say it's a myth. Whatever other people's beliefs might be, I think that if you work hard and put forth your best effort, you can create an extremely successful process. It might not be perfect for everyone, but it will be perfect for *you*, and that's all that matters. Your entire sales journey will, in a way, be a continuous struggle to find *your* highly elusive—yet greatly rewarding—"perfect" sales process.

A sales process is a channel for your skills, a testing ground for your tools and an ongoing project upon which you will continue to improve. With a twist here and a tweak there, your sales process, like wine, gets better with age. Every smart salesperson has a process, whether he knows it or not, whether it's in his subconscious or written down somewhere. You will depend on it; it will become your pathway to success, the gateway through which you let in your dreams. You must feel it rather than rationalize it.

A definitive sales process is a way to realize your full potential and function at the best of your abilities. If you are selling ten cars per month without a defined process, you can sell twenty or even thirty with one. If you put in ten times the effort, you will likely yield ten times the results.

You cannot perform well unless you have mastered the "basics" of car sales, and the process *is* the basics. Without it, you cannot move forward and hope to sell thirty cars in a month. Before we begin creating *your* perfect sales process, let's examine the overall process in more detail.

Sales process—two words around which the whole of your career as a salesperson will revolve. And, if you want to carry this career forward, you must fully understand the meaning behind these two words and realize the weight that they carry. Once you understand the meaning behind them, you need to work hard to carry out the function for which they were created. You must open your mind to all the possibilities and open yourself in order to act upon those possibilities. You need to be prepared to take any reasonable action that brings you closer to the goal.

Your goal is to sell thirty cars per month; the sales process paves the road to that goal. To fully understand the meaning of the term *sales process*, we must break it down into two key components: *sales* and *process*.

When we talk about sales, we describe an act that has been performed throughout human history, through which one creates or buys a product and exchanges the product for money. This is, put simply, what sales is—giving a product in exchange for money. Right?

Not really. Sales, in its most rudimentary form, *may* be an exchange of goods and services for money, and your goal *may* be to earn the most money selling the most products. However, that's a crude understanding of sales that reduces it to its most basic intent. It's like saying that to be human is to eat, drink and reproduce. But just as there's more to being human than merely surviving, there's a lot more to sales than simply selling. If you want to succeed in sales, you need to take a more sophisticated view of the process than that.

Sales is, at its most basic level, not simply a process of selling products. It's a process of providing solutions. Your goal is not merely to earn more by selling more; it's to satisfy the needs of the customer to whom you sell. And, once you realize that crucial distinction, you are at least ready to contemplate the meaning of a process.

What exactly is process? What comes to mind when you think of a process? Is it a system or a set of steps? If you're thinking along these lines, you're closer to the true meaning of the word "process."

When we consider the dictionary definition of the word "process," we discover that a process is, generally, a defined set of steps that naturally lead up to and then follow one another. A process is a systematic way of performing a specific task. The task, in this case, is sales. Therefore, a sales process is a systematic way of selling products in exchange for money while also satisfying the needs of the customer. It's a defined set of steps that brings you closer to your ultimate goal—selling thirty cars per month while creating a base of satisfied customers. This set of steps is not random, however, and they must be repeatable. They form a path on which you can tread not once but again and again. It's easier each time you do it, and it offers newer challenges each time as well.

CREATING A PROCESS

Creating a process is extremely important when it comes time to set out to achieve your sales goals. How you create the process, however, is even more important. The way you think about the process and the way your mindset works is reflected in the look and feel of your final process. The ways in which you perceive your goals, and the ways in which you set out to achieve those goals, are parts of the process.

A good process is a reflection of good values. It's a combination of ideals and a strong work ethic. It's a product of vision combined with skill. Skill and practice can be constant, but vision and ideas are variable, so it's important to further define these concepts.

Your process will likely depend upon your position on the sales team. If you're a manager, your sales process will look entirely different than it would if you were a salesperson. Your number of years of experience help, too. If you're a junior salesperson, your process will be considerably different from that of a senior salesperson. It all depends upon where you stand and how you see your goal from your unique point of view. It also depends upon your preferences as a salesperson and your goals when you set out to achieve your larger objectives. So, all in all, it's safe to say that a process is variable. It's fluid and dynamic.

Depending upon your scope, there are two kinds of processes: the *macro process* and the *micro process*. Let's consider the differences between these two to understand how they differ based on your approach.

The *macro process* depends upon your view of sales in general. It emerges when you see sales as a whole, as a tiny universe in and of itself. The goal of the macro process is simple: sell thirty cars per month. There's little regard for the future, little consideration for the consequences of the actions you take to reach the goal of thirty cars per month.

On the other hand, the *micro process* is created with the finer details of the sales procedure in mind. It takes into account the intricacies of selling. Here, too, the larger goal is to sell thirty cars per month. However, *how* you reach the goal is also important. The micro process focuses on your interactions with each and every customer. Whereas those who utilize only the macro approach believe that results are the most important, the micro process focuses on the consequences of the actions you take to obtain those results. The goal is not simply to sell as many cars as you can. It is to focus on creating a repeat client with each and every sale. It's to pave the way for the future as you carefully tread upon the present.

You can likely guess which of these approaches I prefer, but how do know which approach is the best for you? Some suggest that the best approach is the one that makes you the most money. I (clearly) believe otherwise. You earn money no matter what your priorities are. By thinking long-term, you are securing your future while earning in the present. I favor the more careful approach, one that takes into account the needs of the customers while achieving what you aim to achieve financially.

A good process is not only one that makes you rich but also one that *feels* right instinctively. It's the one that brings you the most satisfaction. Owning the "perfect" process is like slipping into a pair of well-worn shoes. You need to be as comfortable with it as you are in your own skin. A process is nearly perfect for you when each of its individual components comes together in the best possible manner, functioning together like a well-oiled machine.

COMING TO COMMON TERMS: COMPONENTS OF THE PROCESS

No two sales processes are alike. Each has its own identity. Each one's heart beats at a different speed. Every process is the unique manifestation of the personality of the salesperson behind it all. However, despite all the differences in sales processes, there are also commonalities. Regardless of your approach to selling, regardless of your personal preferences, regardless of whether you process is micro or macro, one thing is for certain: each process contains key components.

Each process begins with, or in some way involves, an early stage prospect—a potential customer who is part of the salesperson's target audience. Each process revolves around or somehow involves a way to convert that potential prospect into a sold customer, and each process has an organized set of steps to enable the salesperson to accomplish that goal. Each car sales process focuses on finding the best and most foolproof ways of closing deals and, even though not all processes involve following up with sold customers, those that do are the successful ones. Here's a brief look at the similar components of successful sales processes:

PROSPECT

According to one perspective, every person who hasn't yet walked into your dealership—as well as everyone who crosses the threshold—is a prospect. I'm fine with that belief as long as it works for you. For myself, however, that scope is rather broad as the basis of a comprehensive strategy. Sure, I would *like* every living human being to be a potential prospect, but that is not the case. There are certain identifying characteristics of a true prospect, and once you identify these characteristics you're more capable of closing them.

A person is a prospect if he or she meets these basic criteria:

Buying Authority

Is he the decision maker of the family? Is he the owner of the money with which a car is being purchased? If so, he's the right person to focus on. For instance, if a husband and wife walk into your dealership, in most cases the husband is the one who has the buying authority, and the wife is the influencer. Therefore, the husband is your prospect.

Financial Capacity

Can he afford the vehicle? If so, he should be higher on your list of priorities. If not, you certainly don't have to ignore him, but you also don't need to waste sizeable effort on him.

Willingness to Purchase

Financial capacity and willingness to buy go hand-in-hand. If the customer can afford the vehicle but hasn't the will to buy it, you will need to make more of an effort to bring him to the table. If he has the willingness to buy but not the ability to pay, he is a warmer lead that may take time to turn into a hot lead. If, however, he has *both* the willingness *and* the capacity to buy, he is definitely a target prospect.

CONNECT

Once you are successfully able to identify and classify prospects, it's time to connect with them. There are unlimited ways to connect with prospects and no "right" way. You can use traditional means of approaching each and every prospect and inviting him to buy from you (in other words, attract prospects through the sheer strength of your personality). You can also use non-traditional means such as social media or email.

The manner in which you connect with prospects is also crucial. In order to sell thirty cars per month, the majority of your success will hinge upon how well you're able to connect with prospects. The goal is to influence prospects to buy from you. When you set out to do so, you'll quickly realize how challenging this can be. People are simply not easily influenced! It requires a unique combination of personality and skill, and it's important to follow the ten-to-one rule: for every ten prospects you connect with, only one will end up buying a vehicle. Therefore, in order to gain thirty paying customers, you will need to connect with 300 prospects. Either that, or you better get better at closing!

DEMONSTRATE

When people think of a car salesperson, they typically think of a well-groomed individual in a suit or a tie who explains the various features of a vehicle. This is what your audience expects from you, and this is the key area where you must deliver. When the expectations are so high, you must rise above your ability and deliver a stunning performance. No less than that is required to satisfy the demands of the customer. The perception a customer has of the salesperson while he or she is demonstrating the vehicle is the reason why demonstration is so critical. Therefore, you should spend a large amount of time perfecting this activity.

Despite its huge importance (or maybe because of it), car salespeople often take this step for granted. They think that because they do it many times every day, they don't need to put effort into it, but this is where good salespeople distinguish themselves. They realize the importance of the demonstration and put significant effort into it.

In my twelve years of car sales experience, I put the most effort into my demonstration skills. I used to stand in front of the mirror and practice proper presentation for hours. As I mentioned earlier, I stammered while trying to talk quickly; it was a disadvantage I had to overcome. And I did, through will power alone, in order to achieve my desired results. That only happened, however, once I realized the importance of proper demonstration skills. I never took them for granted, and I never postponed the hard work that was required.

CLOSE

As we have discussed, and will discuss further, it takes a certain level of skill to impress the customer enough that they even consider purchasing a vehicle. It takes an entirely different set of skills to bring them to the table and get them to sign on the dotted line. To be a successful salesperson, you need to be able to demonstrate, but you should also know how to effectively close the deal. You cannot rely on your superiors to do the job every time, and since your goal is to sell thirty cars per month, you need to learn this skill quickly. Sales can be a rapid succession of demonstrate and close, demonstrate and close, demonstrate and close.

You need to be equipped with all the necessary tools, tips and techniques to enable you to effectively close the deal—even before you begin. The most crucial requirement is a constant presence of mind. You need to know when and with which customer to use a particular closing technique. You need to be able to correctly assess where the sales process is going and change tact when necessary. Successful closing involves much more than simply throwing a random set of card tricks at the customer. It requires sharp focus and acquired skill. Although experience teaches you a great deal, you must be prepared to be polishing your skills even as you are just beginning. Don't leave it all to experience. Successful closing is a study in personality; you must be able to read the customer and form a strategy accordingly.

FOLLOW UP

While most sales processes include all of the aforementioned steps, the difference between an average sales process and a successful one is in the follow-up. The follow-up is the one are that can have a huge impact in taking you from selling ten to thirty cars per month.

Your first task as an aspiring salesperson is to understand the importance of a good follow-up. Once you do that, you will work to make it an essential component of your sales process. In addition, the follow-up should fit seamlessly into the process. Most, if not all, of the other components will depend upon the quality of the follow-up since the number of prospects you attract—as well as how many leads you connect with—depends upon the strength of the follow-up.

Follow-up has two different forms. You follow up with prospective leads to increase the amount of walk-in traffic, and you follow up with sold customers to gain loyalty, create repeat clients and build a steady stream of referrals. Both types of follow-up generate a significantly expanded customer base, but each requires a different strategy. You must be well-versed in both strategies in order to consistently sell thirty cars per month.

THE 4 KEYS TO SUCCESSFUL SALES

I'm often asked, "What does it take to sell thirty cars per month?" If you asked me to summarize all that's required to reach this goal, I would tell you to master these four essential steps. Focus all your energies into perfecting your performance in these four key areas, and you'll see surprising results. Roll up your sleeves and shift gears because we're about to get down to the nitty-gritty of successful sales.

When I started out in the car industry, I had no idea how to successfully sell; I had no clear sense of what I needed to do or where I needed to go. I didn't know on which areas I needed to focus my energy, and I was thoroughly unaware of the importance of certain aspects of sales performance. It was years of hard work, making mistakes and learning from those mistakes that led me to separate what was important from what was not. Only then was I able to identify these four crucial areas of the sales machine, and it is on these areas that we must focus.

We must separately examine and analyze each of these four key areas in order to understand what works best and what to avoid. However, there's also a need to identify how they collectively contribute to a successful sales process.

THE SALES PROCESS

The first and most important aspect of successful sales is the sales process itself. It is one of the three pillars (the three

Ps) of sales: People, Product and Process. You cannot even begin to imagine the enormity of the sales process until you divide and sub-divide it into specific steps. Successful sales are only possible when approached in an organized fashion, and this is where a process comes into play. Once you are fully organized and know what you need to do before you do it, it's time to move to the next step.

In order to create a successful sales process, we must first understand what a sales process is. By definition, a sales process is a defined set of steps that you, as a salesperson, need to follow in order to convert an early-stage lead into a sold customer. You follow this series of steps, one at a time, in order to successfully sell a product, and the nature of the process determines the success or failure of the sales procedure.

What does a typical sales process looks like? Truthfully, that depends on the industry. Sales processes may differ depending on the kind of business you're conducting but, additionally, you can also create your own sales process, which can vary from company to company in a similar industry as well as from person to person in a single company. Therefore, it's nearly impossible to identify a one-size-fits-all process. There are, however, elements that can be found in any successful car sales process. These may include looking for prospects, connecting with leads, receiving potential customers on the floor, demonstrating the vehicle, taking the customer on a test drive, closing the deal and following up with the customer.

When you set out to create a sales process, you need to first consider the nature of your business. In the area of car sales, before designing the process you must keep in mind the demands of the industry. You then need to keep a sharp eye on what works and what doesn't in the industry. Observe how other businesses are conducting their affairs. Analyze how their process works for them and what you can do to improve upon it.

Once you create the process, the task isn't over; in fact, it has only just begun. Creating the sales process is merely the first step to success. The real work begins after that, as you continuously improve the sales process through inspiration, learning from others' examples and a steady stream of trial and error. You must also consider the ever-changing dynamics of the car sales business. You need to keep up with current trends in customer preferences and continue to modify the sales process accordingly. Constant review and revision is the necessary prerequisite to a perfect process.

SALESMANSHIP

This is seemingly the most obvious area. After all, that's what we're all here for, right—to improve our salesmanship skills in order to increase our sales numbers? But how exactly do we do that? Are there any tips and tricks that can enable us to be better salespeople? If you're looking for shortcuts to drastically increase your sales numbers, perhaps you need to reconsider your entire approach. There are no shortcuts to the 30-Car Club. It takes immense dedication and hard work to be able to sell thirty cars per month; it's not easy (but it's definitely doable)!

Before we move on to the specific measures that must be taken to improve sales numbers, we need to have a thorough understanding of what salesmanship is and what it takes to be a good salesperson. Simply defined, salesmanship is the ability to convince or persuade a person to buy a particular product.

How well you're able to convince people and the number of people you're able to convince depend upon how good of a salesman you are. Good salespeople don't simply sell a product to the maximum number of people. It's not only about the quantity of sales; it's also about the quality of the service. Good salespeople work hard to make each and every customer's experience special and unique. They have a knack for creating repeat clients out of one-time customers or prospects.

While there are a number of factors involved in creating a good salesperson, it takes a unique combination of natural talent and acquired skills. No one is a born salesman, and no one can simply read books in order develop a successful sales approach. It takes talent as well as acquired skill in equal measure. Apart from having a set of skills, you must also be able to meaningfully use these skills to your advantage.

To be a good salesperson, you must, first and foremost, understand the needs of the customer. This is, in some ways, the most valuable skill you must possess in order to be a successful salesperson. If you're able to truly understand what the customer wants, you can easily deliver it to him and make the sales experience an enjoyable one for the customer. You'll receive referrals and repeat clients, and the cycle will continue.

Apart from being aware of the customer's wishes, you must appear reliable and trustworthy. Customers should feel at ease around you. It's your job to make the customers comfortable enough to trust you and, once you've earned their confidence, you need to deliver a truly spectacular demonstration. When the customers already trust you, they are more likely to believe what you say during the demonstration and be convinced by your arguments. You need to be sociable in order to gain more and more leads, and you must be extremely professional in order to take those prospects to the next stage.

CLOSING THE DEAL

Some salespeople believe that once they give a terrific presentation and bring the customer successfully to the table, their job is over. I want to tell you from the bottom of my heart that that's not true. That's only one half of the sales process. It's *never* over until you close the deal and receive the customer's signature, and there's a lot that can go wrong from the moment the customer agrees to negotiate the price until the moment he takes the car home. This is why successful closing demands so much of a salesperson's attention.

Closing the deal is one of the most critical components of the entire sales process. The success or failure of the entire endeavor depends upon how well you can close, and many dealerships realize the importance of this step. This is the reason I have seen many dealerships assign some of their senior salespeople to be the "closers." When a particular member of the sales team successfully brings a customer to the table, the "closer" is then sent over to successfully seal the deal. Dealerships simply aren't prepared to take a chance on an inexperienced salesperson messing up the deal. That's how critical closing is.

Your sales process must be fluid enough to allow for a smooth closing. It's like preparing yourself for a soft landing after a hard fall. You need to be able to deal with any potential problems that come your way during the closing. This is only possible when you successfully get (and keep) the process in motion. If the customer raises an objection, you need to be able to counter in an instant—not only addressing the specific objection but also fully satisfying the customer. It's like a boxing match. If someone connects with a right hook, you need to be able to instantly counter. Otherwise, prepare to be knocked out.

There are various closing techniques you can implement, and I will discuss some of them later on. Not only do you need to know these techniques, you will also need to be able to use the right technique with the right customer. This is another area that separates a good salesperson from an average one. Anyone can throw a bunch of random closing techniques at a customer, but for these techniques to stick, you need to truly know the customer inside and out. You need a full command of the customer's psyche in order to choose the right technique at the right time.

There are many common closing mistakes you must avoid in order to become a consistent closer. Timing is key to closing the deal, and you must be careful not to attempt to close too early or wait too long. Many salespeople, in their enthusiasm to seal the deal, attack too early. Others continue to talk past the close and end up ruining the deal. These are the kinds of mistakes you need to avoid in order to maximize your closing ratio. The harder you work on improving your sales ratio, the closer you will be to selling thirty cars per month.

THE FOLLOW-UP

As you set out on the path to selling thirty cars per month, you will begin to realize that it's not easy to reach that level. It's even more difficult to sustain sales at that level month-in and month-out. The strain will continue to build as you scramble to find more and more walk-in customers, and you simply won't be able to sustain that number. Your sales numbers will, therefore, go down without warning, and you won't know what hit you.

Fortunately, there's an easy way out of this mess, and that is to maintain regular follow-up with customers. Build a steady stream of referrals, and you'll never again need to worry about the lack of walk-in or repeat clients. The follow-up is the most effective way to sustain your sales numbers because it ensures that you build a loyal customer base. When you reach out to customers *after* they've bought the product, it reinforces trust and the belief in your services that was created in the customer's mind during your most recent interaction. When done effectively, your customers will remember you the next time they set out to shop for a car.

Apart from creating a loyal customer base, you must also seek to expand your customer list through follow-up, which can be done by seeking referral business. The principle is simple. If the customer liked your services, he should be comfortable referring it to others, which will send more customers your way, thereby easily increasing your sales numbers. Many salespeople underestimate the power of referrals or don't bother to ask customers for referrals, and thereby fail without knowing it.

Look at it this way: if all of your customers refer one person (on average) to buy a car from you, you'll double your current number of clients in no time. The average is usually higher than that if you have an effective follow-up process. The referrals who walk in to your dealership will be different from the regular walk-in crowd; it'll be easier to close the sale with them since they are ready to buy and already have a degree of trust in your services.

In addition to following up with existing customers, it's also extremely important to follow up with the leads, prospects and potential clients in your list. Not everyone who wants to buy a car will visit your dealership, and those who do won't be enough. Therefore, you must increase your activity over the phone and contact more leads in order to secure more customers. Calling your leads once is not enough. You need to diligently follow up with each and every one of them in order to achieve the best results.

Repetition and consistency are the key requirements. You need to be unrelenting in your efforts to secure each and every customer. You must be systematic in your approach to follow-up. Be organized. Maintain notes. There's a lot to do in this area and a whole world of possibilities to explore. In the end, you must settle on the approach that yields the best results for you and your customers.

THE 10 STEPS OF A SUCCESSFUL SALES PROCESS

Now that we have discussed the sales process at a high level, we must turn our attention to the actual process itself. I've used and honed the following 10-step process over the years to produce razor-sharp results. You certainly don't have to follow this process to a tee. You can absolutely create your own process from scratch to be suited to your specific needs. I recommend that you simply use this process as a template to launch yourself into the 30-Car Club, and make necessary changes as you go.

MEET AND GREET

"You don't get a second chance to make a first impression."
– James Uleman

The meet and greet is where it all starts. As the customer walks into the dealership, it's time to stop thinking about the best ways to impress him and start acting upon the impulse to do so. The meet and greet is its own step; you simply cannot ignore it or take it for granted. It's your first chance to make a great impression on the customer, and you won't get a second chance.

To the customer, the meet and greet may be an ordinary part of the routine, but it's a ritual that you need to practice again and again in order to perfect it. When it comes to the meet and greet, I advise you to avoid two common approaches. First, do not wing it. Second, do not be fully aware of the importance of the meet and greet but, and your desperation to impress the customer right off the bat, freak out and make a fool of yourself.

The key to a great meet and greet is to relax and be moderate in your approach. Don’t be over-enthusiastic, and don’t be cold. Don’t attack customers as they step out of their vehicle, but don't linger and ignore them, either. A perfect greeting is all about finding that important balance.

FACT FINDING

In my opinion, sales is the process of simultaneously selling a product for money while satisfying the customer. But how exactly can you satisfy a customer if you don’t even know what he wants? If there’s one thing that separates great salespeople from mediocre ones, it’s the full understanding of each customer's needs and the commitment to doing his best to meet those needs.

The process through which you attempt to discover what the customer is after is called fact finding; you ask the customer a series of questions in order to determine exactly what he needs. Many customers are simply not expressive enough. They want the sales person to know, by default, what they're looking for. Your job, as a good salesperson, is to identify what he wants by extracting the required information through the right questions.

Fact-finding questions vary considerably, but their purpose is always the same. Some examples:

- What budget do you have in mind?

- What features are you not willing to give up?
- What have you had before that you would like to have again?
- What features are nice-to-haves versus must-haves?
- What would you like to have in your next vehicle that you don't have now?
- What are your plans for your current vehicle?
- Did you finance your current vehicle or pay cash for it?

These questions give you an initial data set to which you can refer back at any point during the rest of the process. It's quite possibly the most valuable information you will receive.

VEHICLE SELECTION

If there's one step that is as important as the demonstration of the vehicle (if not more so), it's vehicle selection. Your goal is to satisfy the customer, and the journey begins from this point. When it comes to vehicle selection, the most important thing to remember is that it's the customer's choice that matters, not yours. You have to place yourself in *the customer's* shoes. You must think like your customer and forget all about the vehicle that you've perhaps been assigned to sell. You can't ram a specific vehicle down your customer's throat; if you do so, and the customer ends up buying it, he won't be happy in the long run.

Here, too, you must rely on the data set you procured early on. Narrow down the list of choices based on what the customer is looking for in a vehicle. If the vehicle you're assigned to sell matches his want and needs, you're a lucky duck. If not, focus on selling him the kind of vehicle *he* wants.

A good salesperson acts as the eyes and ears of his customers—that's his job.

PRESENTATION AND DEMO

Here we are at the big moment. The presentation/demo is the most important step in the sales process and the one to which you should pay the most attention. Begin working on your presentation and demo skills long before the customer walks into the dealership. If the perfect demonstration is an art (and it is), you must treat the perfection of it as an art form that requires a combination of talent and hard work.

The demonstration should neither be too short, such that the customers aren't satisfied, nor should it be too long, causing customers to become bored and overwhelmed by too much information. If you know a lot about a specific vehicle, save excess information for the Q&A portion of the process. On average, the presentation time should be kept to around ten minutes. You have to present all the *relevant* information to the customer within those ten minutes.

The walk-around is usually broken down into six steps:

1. Begin at the front of the vehicle. Explain its features, such as aerodynamic shape.
2. Explain the key features of the engine. You can lift the hood open if you'd like.
3. Move to the passenger side of the vehicle, and open the doors while explaining the side features.
4. Move to the back of the vehicle and explain the rear and trunk.
5. Move to the driver's side, and open the doors.
6. Seat the customer in the driver seat, and explain the internal features.

Remember: 80% on your feet, 20% in your seat. Spend more time on this concept, and negotiations will begin to take care of themselves.

TRIAL CLOSE

Now that you have fully captivated the customer's attention, it's time for the first trial close. This is the point at which Phase One of the sales process ends and Phase Two begins. This is the time to ask the customer whether or not he's ready to move to the next step—purchasing the vehicle.

The demonstration and trial close work hand-in-hand. During the demonstration, ask the customer subtle questions such as:

- Are the seats comfortable enough for you?
- Are you satisfied with the vehicle's safety features?
- Are you happy with the smoothness of the ride?

  If the answers are all "Yes," move on to the *real* questions you've been building toward:

- Is this the right vehicle for you?
- Is it perfect for your needs?

If the answers to these questions are also "Yes," the deal is 90% in the bag. If the answer is "No," you should return to the previous step and once again build to the trial close.

TRADE-IN EVALUATION

This is the stage from which the process begins to pick up speed. Now you're moving toward concrete action rather than simply having a back-and-forth exchange of information. If the customer has agreed to enter this stage, it means he is fully willing to buy the vehicle. It's your responsibility to correctly execute the sale from this point forward.

Asking for trade-in is crucial; how you ask for it is also important. Even if the customer seems slightly unwilling, remind him that he doesn't *have* to exchange his vehicle, but a simple evaluation can't hurt. This is a solid way to bring an unwilling customer to at least consider the possibility of a trade-in.

WRITE UP

Once the trade-in (if applicable) is complete and the process is moving toward a more formal step, you must put on your business-like persona. This certainly doesn't mean that you must drop your friendly demeanor; it simply means that you must be much more analytical and systematic. The best way to do that is through a write-up. A write-up, commonly known in the industry as the "foursquare write-up," is a document with four distinct sections. You need to fill in these sections in order to present the customer with an overview of his situation.

The key components of a foursquare write-up are:

SELLING PRICE

When writing up the selling price, enter the full manufacturer's suggested retail price (MSRP) in the price column. This is the price point from which negotiations begin.

TRADE-IN VALUE/ALLOWANCE

When presenting the customer with a trade-in offer, remember to begin with information that supports *your* offer. The goal is to pull the customer as far in the direction of your offer as possible.

DOWN-PAYMENT

When settling on a down-payment, your goal is to extract as much of a down-payment as possible in order to get the best approval rate.

MONTHLY PAYMENT

This is the number upon which most negotiations occur. Remember, the customer is more concerned about how much he'll be paying per month than with the total price of the vehicle. Even the slightest increase in the monthly payment can make a huge impact.

NEGOTIATE AND CLOSE

At this point, it's time to drop any pretenses and move in for the close. The write-up is a critical stepping-stone to this step, but in the final close you must remember to keep the negotiations as far away from the vehicle's *total* selling price as possible.

It's important to understand the "hit-figure"—the figure from which you started the negotiations. It's always higher than the amount on which you want to settle. If you want to settle high, keep the hit-figure higher. If you want to settle low, the hit-figure should be well below the value at which you started.

PROPER TURN TO BUSINESS OFFICE

It's time to make the sale official! Regardless of the agreement on which you informally settled, it's time to put it into writing. This step involves securing necessary documents and following formal procedures. Most of this work can be handled by the finance and insurance departments. You should not, however, abandon the customer. It is your job to make the transition of the vehicle from the dealership to the customer as smooth as possible.

DELIVERY

When all is said and done, your relationship with the customer does not end. In fact, it has only just begun. The effectiveness of your post-delivery services is critical in determining the terms of the relationship going forward. It's important to attempt to create a repeat client, and your delivery of the vehicle is the first step in that direction.

Even if your dealership employs a dedicated delivery coordinator, you must still play an active role in the delivery process. In order to avoid any unnecessary problems or glitches, it's better to work off of a delivery checklist. Get your hands dirty. Inspect the vehicle as though *you* own it. Make sure the gas tank is full when the vehicle leaves the dealership. It's the little things that make a huge impact on the customer and keeps him coming back to you and sending more referrals your way.

10 Sales Mistakes to Avoid Like the Plague

FORGET TO ASK QUALIFYING QUESTIONS

One of the biggest mistakes a car salesperson can commit is not asking qualifying questions. Qualifying questions are a set of simple questions you ask the customer to determine whether or not he can afford the vehicle in the first place.

Many salespeople, in their haste to make the sale, forget to begin with this crucial step. Others, in an effort to avoid appearing hawkish, ignore this step entirely. Both approaches are equally disastrous.

You absolutely *must* ask the qualifying questions. Your goal is not simply to determine the customer's financial capability. You also need to know the kind of vehicle the customer is looking for or the features the customer wants in a vehicle. When you don't start with this step, you waste valuable time—and time is money.

BEGIN THE SALES PITCH RIGHT AWAY

Remember the introductory sales speech you likely memorized in front of the mirror recently? Delete it from your memory; you don't need it. Your customers *definitely* don't need it. No one wants to be showered with information before they've even entered the dealership.

The meet and greet phase is your first real chance to make an impression on the customer. Don't mess it up by appearing to be a sleazy, clingy salesperson. It is crucial to give the customer some time to gather his thoughts and become accustomed to his environment. There will be time for the sales pitch later.

OFFER TOO MUCH OR TOO LITTLE INFORMATION ABOUT THE VEHICLE

When you demonstrate the vehicle, your goal is to educate the customer about some of the vehicle's features. There's a limit, however, to how much the customers like to know, and it's your job to maintain the critical balance between too much and too little information.

The customer's goal is not to earn a degree. You don't need to overburden him with excessive technical details. Save your intricate knowledge of the vehicle for the enthusiasts who may genuinely be interested in those details about the vehicle. If someone asks about a particular detail, you can certainly discuss the technical aspects. Otherwise, focus on keeping the demonstration short and relevant.

On the other hand, customers don't appreciate being given so little information that they cannot make up their minds. Some car salespeople move around the vehicle stating the obvious. If the customers already know everything you're about to tell them, what exactly is the point of the demonstration?

BLABBER ON AND ON

No one appreciates a salesperson who never shuts up.

It is not your obligation to fill silences by constantly droning on about offers, services and features of the vehicle. It is a common misconception in sales that selling is a one-way communication where a salesperson talks and the customer listens. Let me assure you, that's not true.

Instead, selling is a two-way conversation. Your job is not simply to blabber on and on but also to listen to the customer's questions and concerns and ask him questions as well. Salespeople often forget or dismiss the value of silence. It's important to offer the customer the crucial commodity of silence so that he can make the decision in peace.

POSTPONE THE PRICE DISCUSSION

Perfectly presenting a vehicle is hard work, and no one knows that better than a salesperson. After all, you wouldn't enjoy spending your precious time demonstrating every feature of a vehicle, asking and answering questions, overcoming objections and satisfying all of the customer's concerns only to find out that the vehicle was way out of the customer's budget to begin with, would you?

To avoid this, always discuss the price of the vehicle before the demonstration, during the meet and greet phase. Remember, that is the phase during which you get to know everything you need to know about the customer, and one of the most important of those things is his price range. Never begin the demonstration before you are absolutely sure that the customer can afford the vehicle.

IGNORE INFLUENCERS

If a customer arrives at the dealership alone, you can ignore this step entirely, but that does not usually happen. Customers typically come in pairs or groups. Within that group, one of the customers is the decision maker (the one who carries the cash). The others are the influencers, and they are there to support or object to the decision maker's decision.

Many salespersons commit the unforgivable mistake of selling only to the decision maker and ignoring the influencers. *Never* do that. The influencers can be your most valuable resource and can prove to be instrumental in convincing the decision maker where you may have fallen short.

IGNORE WHAT THE CUSTOMER WANTS

If you're going to ignore the customer's wishes, what is the point of trying to sell to him? Customers want to buy what *they* want to buy, not what *you* want to sell them. Their wants are your most important consideration—it's all that matters.

Nevermind your sales bonuses on particular vehicles or special discount offers or promotions. Listen carefully to what the customer has to say. If any of the products that you're asked to push matches the customer's wishes, by all means suggest them. But don't ram your preferred products down his throat. He may agree to buy what you want to sell him (against his better judgment), but he won't ever come back.

BE TOO AGGRESSIVE

This is another of the "sales strategies" others claim produces results. People may tell you that selling 100 cars in a month is difficult and that, to achieve that, you must appear hungry and show that hunger to the customers. Actually, you don't need to do anything of the sort.

In fact, you need to avoid such behavior altogether. Avoid hounding the customers and selling too aggressively. Aggressiveness can work wonders in sports, but in sales you need to follow a rational approach. You need to be calm at all times despite how desperately you want to sell the vehicle. Let the customer know how important his is, but don't bully him into buying a product. This is one of the methods that can artificially boost sales numbers, but ultimately it destroys your reputation and scares away potential repeat clients.

IGNORE THE FOLLOW-UP

Your customers are your most valuable resource. Not only do they pay your salary and commissions through purchasing vehicles, they are also the foundation upon which your organization stands. Your dealership runs on the repeat business opportunities they provide. Even more significant than that is their potential to bring other customers to your dealership.

One of the steps through which you ensure that each customer returns to buy from you again and again, as well as that each customer brings other customers along, is the follow-up. The follow-up is crucial for a variety of reasons. A good follow-up leads to improved customer satisfaction ratings. It helps in maintaining and growing a steady repeat client base. It also rakes in referrals.

Each customer has the potential to bring in ten more customers, and those ten customers can bring in even more. Your goal is to enable that chain to continue and prevent it from breaking at any point along the way. If you ignore the follow-up, you not only lose the customer, you lose those ten potential future customers they might refer as well.

FORGET TO SEEK NEWER CLIENTS

Once you are comfortably selling thirty cars per month, customers continue to walk in and you have managed to consistently sustain your sales numbers—maybe even years—is it the time to settle down comfortably and rake in the cash? Not quite. Your search for newer clients is a never-ending one. Remember that thirty cars per month is not your be-all-end-all. It was merely your *initial* goal. You can continue to grow well beyond that, but that is only possible through seeking out newer clients.

Another reason to continue to expand your customer base is to provide much-needed security to your business. In the case of an economic crisis, you must have enough customers to keep you going through the tough spots. Even if you're the most successful dealership in town, it can all quickly crumble like a house of cards. To prevent that, continue to seek new clients regularly.

Salesmanship

* * *

Salesmanship is a rather abstract concept—a vague umbrella term that is made up of many different views on how to sell products. Everyone has his own beliefs and methods. Everyone has a different story to tell. And perhaps the sheer number of sometimes-contradictory views on salesmanship is a testament to *why* it is an integral component of a sales process. In order to sell thirty cars per month, you must have good salesmanship skills. What, exactly, makes you a good salesperson? The answer to that question is precisely where views and opinions begin to diverge.

What makes a good salesperson? is an age-old question that has perturbed generations of salespeople. What is required to succeed in this (or any) industry? These are valuable starting points for discussion, and they can act as a sort of diving board—a platform from which to plunge into the deep mysteries of salesmanship success. We'll use these questions as the basis of our search for ways to significantly increase your daily and monthly sales figures.

If one takes a simplistic view of salesmanship, he could suggest (as he could with regard to the sales process) that a good salesperson is one who sells the most products. According to this view, it's not important to gauge skills or examine techniques. It simply provides an easy way to determine, at end of month, who is good and who is not.

On one level, this definition may be appealing. After all, isn’t good salesmanship simply earning the most money by selling the most products? If so, we needn't go any deeper to analyze the dynamics of good salesmanship. It's interesting that many businesses that appear robust and successful have adopted this view.

I, however, don’t.

This is, quite frankly, a much too elementary and simplistic view of sales and caveman-like in its approach. When we reduce sales down to its most basic, primitive purpose of buying and selling and making money, we ignore the beautiful complexities and delicate intricacies involved in the process. We rob our young people of the chance to benefit from and build upon years of hard work by much greater salespersons who preceded us. This is a regressive approach rather than progressive and, I assure you, we can be much more successful by having a broader view of salesmanship.

Salesmanship is the complex system of interlinked skills and techniques associated with the sales process. It’s a multifaceted system of not only selling products to earn money but also offering solutions to those in need. Good salesmanship involves much more than selling the highest number of products. It involves understanding a customer’s needs and addressing those needs in order to offer specific solutions that solve their problem. Salesmanship is a collection of values you must embrace in order to succeed in selling the most products.

I say this not simply from a moralistic view of doing customers a service. My model is also a highly practical one. We run a business, not a charity. As such, our goals as salespeople must be to expand the business as far as possible and generate as much revenue as possible, and the path to business success is created through customer satisfaction.

This is precisely what many up-and-coming businesses sadly fail to understand. They focus all of their energy on generating revenue, not serving customers. They do generate revenue, and a lot of it, but only for a limited amount of time. This may give them the *illusion* of success, but that's far from the long-term reality of the situation. While using cheap tactics to succeed, they don't realize that their customers are slipping. They never focus on building a firm foundation on which to stand. Businesses are not built on huge piles of money alone. They are built on goodwill and trust and a healthy relationship between the business and its customers. Many emerging businesses don't understand that, so as they continue to soar, the ground slips away beneath their feet and they fall. Hard.

Using "shady" business practices in order to boost sales is one of the reasons why huge business ventures suddenly crash—seemingly to everyone's surprise. They don't have solid foundations, so they're hollowed out from the inside. When the weight of their client base's unfulfilled expectations begin to bear down on them, their foundations cannot bear it and they collapse.

My approach is the exact opposite of this. If you, as a salesperson, want to stay employed and simultaneously enjoy success and stability, you must ditch the "sleazy" salesman attire and attitude and never again go near it.

Being a professional salesperson who is sympathetic to the customer's concerns will work wonders for you as well as the business organization for which you work and the clients you hope to serve. The approach is win-win-win. I call it the stable success model, and it requires work to achieve. You must work on your demonstration skills, develop your social skills and approach each and every prospect—individually, if need be—in order to build a client base. The journey will take longer than that of the "sleazy" salesman next door but, I guarantee you, it won't ever fail you.

7 CRITICAL SALESMANSHIP SKILLS

With the aforementioned advice in mind, let's consider the skills required to be a truly good salesperson. Some of these skills are natural, like sociability. Others are acquired through dedication and hard work. Don't get me wrong; I'm not saying that some people are born salespersons while others are not. Don't lose hope if *none* of these skills comes naturally to you. Hard work *always* pays off. I've seen many salespeople who are reserved or shy. However, as soon as they step on the sales floor, they're on fire. They're in their element, and they can drop their shy persona in an instant.

If, while going through this list, you realize that you don't have many of the skills required to be a good salesperson, don't be disappointed. Instead, commit to working hard to develop each skill and hone them to position you as a future star in the industry.

BE A GOOD LISTENER

There is a misconception within the car sales community that, in order to be a successful salesperson, you need to be a great talker—talking a great deal, impressing the customer with your eloquence and ensuring that they can't resist buying your product. Let's suppose you give such an impressive presentation that it convinces the customer that buying the vehicle will solve all his problems, and he buys right away. You pocket the cash, and the customer drives away with the vehicle. What next? When he begins to *use* the vehicle, which wasn't right for him in the first place, you won't be there to talk him into it. He'll feel cheated. And he'll never come back. You will have lost a customer.

Many salespeople don't realize that a good salesperson's job is not simply to talk; it's also to listen. Being a thorough listener and an astute observer are two of most important skills you can hone. In the previous chapter, we discussed the sales process. Go through the process once again, and notice that listening is an integral component of each step.

Take the demonstration, for example. Everyone believes that the demonstration is about eloquent communication. Few claim that you, as the salesperson, need to be listening during a demo. I strongly suggest otherwise. Demonstration, like any other sales communication, is a two-way process. Presenting the rehearsed demo does not require a great amount of skill. The real skill lies in being able to observe the customer's subtle signals of approval or disapproval while you're in the middle of speaking.

EFFECTIVELY ADDRESS THE CUSTOMER'S NEEDS

What is the point of listening if not to address the customer's concerns? The importance of listening is a point to which I return again and again. Without thirty trusting customers every month, you can't hope to sell thirty cars. The customer is your most valuable commodity. Continuing to lose customers is the equivalent of throwing money down the drain, and no one wants to do that. The easy way out of the conundrum is to make the customers—rather than the sales targets—the focus of all your attention. If you run after the customers, your sales targets will automatically scramble after you to catch up.

As a good salesperson, it's not your job to impose your will upon the customer. Your job is to assist the customer in realizing his *own* will. Once you take this approach, you'll see your sales numbers begin to significantly increase. Not only will you generate repeat clients, you'll also get referral business. You must ask more questions than you give answers. What made the customer choose your dealership? What is he looking for in the perfect vehicle? What is his price range? What does he like or dislike about your service? How would he improve upon it? It's critically important to understand your customers without an agenda.

BE SOCIABLE AND HAVE AN EASY-GOING NATURE

Have you ever seen a successful salesperson who seems cold and distant? Probably not. You can be either successful or cold and distant, but you can't be both. You *need* to be sociable and friendly in order to survive in this industry.

Being sociable doesn't mean that you have to be a life-of-a-party kind of person. It means that you have to be approachable and someone with whom people feel at ease.

If you are naturally sociable and have the gift of connecting with people, then that will give you an advantage over those who aren't. If your personality is nothing like that, however, I don't want you to be discouraged. You can work on mastering the impulse to resist contact and be introverted. I am living proof that it's possible. Although I was not what you would call shy or introverted before I entered the car sales industry, I've noticed a huge change in my personality since becoming a salesperson. I'm more outgoing and approachable than ever before, simply because I worked on it.

HONE YOUR PRESENTATION SKILLS

Presentation skills are crucial, and they're also the skills on which you can work the hardest. Having great presentation skills means having the ability to break down complex subjects into easily digestible tidbits for your customers. You have to be an effective communicator to get your message across and let it sink its teeth into the customers' brains. You need to compel their inner desires to inspire them to say, "This is what I want to buy, and I won't buy it anywhere else."

You need to be captivating, mesmerizing even. Your customers always have the choice not to listen to what you have to say, but you need to be able to connect with them on-the-spot so that they don't have a chance *not* to hear what you have to say. There are many ways of working on your presentation skills. You can stand in front of the mirror and speak. You can record yourself and listen. You can gather an audience of friends and family and communicate with them. A fun approach is what I call "playing the game in hard mode." Have your friends raise all kinds of objections and offer all kinds of distractions while you speak. How you dispel those objections and manage those distractions will determine how strong of a presenter you are and how much stronger you become.

STRENGTHEN YOUR PRODUCT KNOWLEDGE

This is another critical sales skill and one that requires a precarious balance between knowing too much about the product and trying to tell the customer everything you know. Let me make it simple. You need to have extensive knowledge of the product if you want to impress the customer and satisfy his needs. However, you also must hold back a lot of the information if you don't want to bore them out of their minds.

Here's the fun question: which pieces of information do you present, and which do you hold back? I like to think that when presenting the same vehicle to 100 different customers, no two of those presentations should be alike. Customers are incredibly smart and perceptive, and they will realize in an instant if you are giving a generic, learned-by-heart presentation. They will also notice when you're telling them exactly what they want to hear (and how much they want to hear). This is why listening to the customer helps you shape your presentation while you're giving it. For instance, if the customer appears to be interested in the vehicle's safety features, speak in-depth about the particular safety measures he'll get with each vehicle. If he's more interested in the engine, by all means go crazy talking about the engine. Impress him with your technical acumen. You can have a lot of fun if you know exactly what you're selling, and that's why you need to be the pinnacle of product knowledge.

BUILD STRONG CUSTOMER RELATIONSHIPS

When you're a salesperson and it's your job to interact with people on a daily basis, chances are that you'll see almost everything and meet nearly every type of person. You'll deal with all kinds of personalities and be expected to handle them with the same amount of care. In order to do that, I find it helpful to classify customers according to four basic personality types. This is called the *DECS technique*. The four personality types and the way to manage each of them are:

Dominant/Driver

"Drivers" are customers who like to feel that they're in control. They want to dominate every interaction and steer the conversation in the direction they want to go. The key to effectively managing this personality type is to hold your ground and never back down. They like and respect assertive people, and you must be one of those people in order to be effective.

Egoist/Expressive

The Egoist's/Expressive's most defining trait is, ironically, your greatest advantage. You simply have to stroke their ego. Keep a stack of sincere complements handy, praise their decisiveness and admire their knowledge. But know when to stop as well! You don't need to appear *too* flattering.

Complacent/Amiable

Complacent/amiable people are extremely friendly. It's easy to sell to them, and you have a chance of developing a great working relationship with them. Connect with them not as a business person but as a human being. You have to sell them on your personality rather than a vehicle. And, if they like what you offer, you'll have yourself a repeat client.

Stable/Analytical

The stable/analytical customers are the thinkers. Analytical people like to take their time to analyze and assess each and every aspect of the decision they're making. They follow a decision-making system and method, and you need to think like them in order to work with them. You'll have greater success using a visual approach. Make a chart or a list of pros and cons. Reach the analytical part of their brain, and you'll find results.

PROPERLY HANDLE OBJECTIONS

Handling objections is one of the less desirable components of salesmanship, but it's one you must deal with all the same. If you put some effort into it, you may even begin to enjoy it. Questions and objections can be fun. Every question is a challenge, and every objection is an opportunity. If you want to close the most deals, you must rise up to every challenge and grab hold of every opportunity. Embrace these questions and objections with an open heart, and you'll never feel trapped by them.

Here are some recommended approaches:

Listen

Some salespeople have a filter that causes them to temporarily go deaf when a question or objection is raised. This is due to the fact that they don't like to operate outside their comfort zone. If you want to be a good salesperson, you need to listen to exactly what the customer says. Listening to the questions and objections will offer you insight into the customer's mindset and allow you the opportunity to frame the exact kind of response he wants.

Explore

You don't have to be a silent observer as the customer raises questions and makes demands. You can ask your own questions to clarify his points. One simple way to do this is to restate the customer's question by paraphrasing it. This gives the customer the impression that you care about his concerns and want to understand in order to help.

Address

This is the phase during which you provide the actual solution. Now that you know exactly what the customer's question is, you also know exactly how to answer. Be patient. Never lose the smile or the friendly demeanor. If you don't know the answer, don't panic. Write the question down, and don't forget to address it later.

Move On

Once you've answered the customer's question and addressed his objection, don't linger on the topic. This can make the customers uncomfortable. Instead, move on to other subjects.

Experience is all about learning from mistakes, but no one would suggest that you *have* to make the mistakes yourself in order to learn something from them. The most successful salespeople learn from the mistakes of others as often as their own. Just as you should know the most common sales skills and techniques to employ, you should also know those to avoid.

The Importance of Knowing Your Numbers

Car sales is a numbers game, and if you want to succeed, you must become the master of those numbers. You must do the math and be prepared to face challenges before you yield results. Success, in car sales, is not an abstract concept connected to your sense of achievement and fulfillment. It's concrete and quantifiable. You need to have a definitive measure of the success you achieve, and this is where numbers come in. These numbers not only help you achieve success, they also help you know the level of success you've achieved.

To make it as simple as possible, there are two major steps to achieving the success you desire. First, you need to set goals for yourself. These should be the *right* goals, the goals that lead you exactly where you want to go. Second, you need to find ways of moving closer and closer to those goals while knowing where you stand at any given moment.

A traditional mindset might suggest that you need to work hard, day and night, to achieve your goals. After all, working hard is a requirement for success, right? It is. However, there are more requirements for success in car sales than simply working hard. You must also work smart, which you do by knowing the numbers, by knowing precisely where you are at any given moment as well as where you need to be. You set targets for yourself as well as milestones along the way to those targets. You must know and follow these numbers like a pro. Your level of success depends on how much you take charge of your situation.

WHAT ARE THE NUMBERS, EXACTLY?

There are two components to numbers: knowing then and knowing how to do your math. In simple terms, your numbers are the sales targets that you need to achieve in a set period of time. For instance, thirty cars in a month is a number. But "sell thirty cars in a month" does not, in and of itself, give you much direction. Even though it's the most important number you need to know, it's also somewhat vague because it doesn't *tell* you anything nor does it lead you anywhere. It simply exists.

It's therefore obvious that there's more to knowing your numbers than simply knowing your sales target. The more relevant set of numbers is the sales metrics. These are the values that contribute to a fully informed sales process. You need to keep track of your sales activities, and these sales metrics help you do that.

Sales metrics come in various shapes and sizes—there is a separate one for each sales activity. You must have a number to represent and inform every step of your sales process. For instance, let's divide the average sales process into three basic steps: calling leads and reaching potential customers through advertising and promotions, receiving customers on the floor and, finally, closing the deal.

These three steps will drive three corresponding values: the number of potential customers you reach in the pre-sales phase, the numbers of customers you receive on the sales floor and the number of customers with whom you close the deal. You will know how close (or how far) you are from your sales goals by keeping track of these numbers. Once you have a record of these numbers, you will begin to see trends. For instance, is walk-in traffic going up or down in successive months? Are you closing more or fewer deals in successive months? And so on.

You can also break your larger sales numbers down even further to help you get a more reliable measure of your sales process by focusing on specific aspects of it. For instance, you have the base number of people with whom you do business in a month. Let's assume you do business with forty customers in a month. "Forty customers" is, on its own, still a broad number, so it's important to break it down further. Of those forty customers, to how many did you demonstrate a vehicle? How many went for a test drive? How many finally closed the deal? Now, instead of looking at simply the number of customers you received in a month, you have more specific data on that set of customers.

QUANTITATIVE DATA

Compiling the numbers in a single place is actually an enjoyable experience! You get to see trends emerging as you plot the numbers, but that's also the point at which you see each number on its own, independent of other variables. The real fun begins when the numbers begin to interact with each other.

Think of your number sheet as a miniature model of the universe. Some numbers revolve around, and depend upon, their fellow numbers. Other numbers travel throughout the matrix and cross each other like galaxies. And other numbers interact with one another and affect their counterparts. New numbers are born like planets as old ones are extinguished like dying stars. It's a beautiful image if we're truly talking about the universe, but the difference is that, as a salesperson, you're at the helm of the way in which these numbers interact with and affect one another.

You observe—and sometimes create—relationships between separate numbers. You begin to notice correlations and causations. You see probabilities and possibilities. For instance, can you see a correlation between the number of customers you call and the number of walk-in customers you receive? Could calling more people lead to more walk-in traffic? What if you called fewer people? Would you receive less traffic? Will you make fewer sales?

Are you feeling like a scientist yet? That's exactly what this process is like. You'll experiment with various values and then compare and contrast the results. You'll suggest the remedies, and then you'll test those remedies.

But if you want to be spot-on in your calculations, you'll need data—and lots of it. This data can be both quantitative and qualitative. Let's begin with quantitative values. Quantitative data begins with good old record keeping. You need to have a living, breathing database of customers. The database should contain not only customers' names, numbers and addresses (as typical databases do) but also customers' entire dealership history—when they came in, what they bought, how many times they were contacted for follow-up and what kind of response they had. This data should be enhanced by detailed notes on every customer that contain every bit of interaction you had with them, including their personal preferences and appointment details.

Keeping track of customers was extremely important to my team and me. That's one of the reasons we set out to create a database-mining tool. After hours and hours spent with our IT team combined with the diligent efforts of my colleague, James DiMeo Jr., we created our own personalized customer database-mining tool, The Autominer (http://www.theautominer.com). The Autominer helped us target customers in unique ways in order to increase retention. With the help of this tool, we were able to make repeat clients out of one-time customers. We followed up with customers and kept track of the progress through The Autominer.

We currently have more than 140,000 customers in the database, and each customer is valuable to us. I have worked hard to cultivate this resource, and it has far exceeded my expectations. With The Autominer, we were not only able to target the right customers; we were also able to perform completely automated database marketing. For instance, it was easier to single out customers who purchased a particular kind of vehicle and then re-target them on the basis of their preferences. It helped me keep track of the numbers but—even more than that—enabled me to capitalize on those numbers and use them to my advantage.

I created The Autominer to do the math *for* me. It was designed to streamline processes that would otherwise take twice my time—and still not be as effective. When I set out to create the tool, I had two clear goals in my mind: simplify the target market and increase customer retention. I wanted to achieve the best results with the least amount of effort, and The Autominer allows me to do that. It allows me to perform a quick and timely search for the right customers; filter search results based on client or date; print, send and export emails and messages; and create customer lists and work plans—all while scheduling, tracking and making calls.

Another factor you must be aware of when compiling your numbers and setting your goals is your working schedule. For instance, if you sell in Texas, you cannot sell on Sundays. Therefore, there are only 26 selling days in a typical month. If you decide to take four days off, you are left with only 22 days to hit your targets.

The math that enables you to hit those targets effectively is called the 4-3-2-1 Rule. In any given working day, you need to:

- Deal with: 4 Customers
- Perform: 3 Demos
- Make: 2 Write-ups
- Carry out: 1 Sale

If you can do this every day, you will sell 22 cars per month. Therefore, in order to get to thirty or better, you need to follow this simple yet effective two-step process:

Get in Front of More Customers

This can be achieved several ways, but what I used to do was try to fill up my pipeline and make sales in every one of the above categories. Once you get dialed in, you'll see that you can sell more than thirty cars relatively easily, but you'll have to be consistent with your follow-up.

Sell 5 customers in every one of these categories:

- Walk-in
- Internet
- Phone calls
- Service
- Referrals
- Prospecting

Improve Your Closing Skills

I highly recommend that you read *The Closer's Survival Guide* by Grant Cardone to learn everything there is to know about effectively closing a deal. You must be so fluid in your responses that they are delivered naturally, just like breathing, and require little-to-no thought. Train like a prizefighter in this area for sure.

QUALITATIVE DATA

For a sound analysis of a sales strategy's success, you cannot rely simply on numbers; quantitative values alone aren't enough. You also need qualitative data. The two go hand-in-hand. Quantitative data shows you whether or not a particular method is working.

For instance, your numbers might show a huge gap between the number of customers you receive and the number of deals you close on any particular day, letting you know that you need to close more customers. This tells you that there is something wrong with your sales process, but perhaps you can’t quite put your finger on what that "something" is. In order to do that, you need qualitative data and, to obtain that, you must turn to your ultimate resource: the customers themselves.

Yes, your customers are also a source of data. In fact, they are the most *important* source of data. Many sales analysts and statisticians get so deeply mired in the intricacies of their data tools that they forget that the simplest way to identify any problem is by simply walking up and asking the customer for feedback. It's a highly effective and underrated method of gathering data. If customers aren't buying your products, who better to learn from than the customers themselves?

Simply approach the customer, and ask what aspect of your sales process he doesn't like. He may not, for example, be impressed by your demonstration. Or, he may have an objection to your negotiation process.

I bet you're thinking, "Yes, what the customer says is important, but I cannot follow the whims and fancies of every single customer. No matter what I do, I cannot keep everyone happy. I cannot cater to everyone; if I do, I'll have no sales process because I'll be changing one thing or another on a daily basis." Important though it is to keep the customers happy, changing your approach on a daily basis is absolutely unadvisable, so what else can you do?

Fortunately, there's a simple way around this challenge. You must increase your sample size—considerably. Where you previously asked questions of ten customers, you must now ask 100. Gather a considerable amount of data before formally analyzing it. Once you have a large enough sample size, you will begin to see patterns. For example, if 90 out of 100 customers think that you need to improve your demonstrative skills, you obviously do.

The scenario becomes a bit trickier when you don't have a clear consensus. Some customers may complain about price while others take issue with the lack of promotions and discounts, providing you with a split opinion. You still, however, have two clear areas for improvement. Even if you have three or four, any number of clear areas in which to improve is better than waving blindly in the dark, indiscriminately trying to change everything all at once.

Soliciting customer feedback is not a one-time exercise. You receive criticism from customers and then return to them with an improved sales process. In addition, customer preferences may change over time. For instance, price can be of more importance to customers during a recession or economic disturbance than at any other time. Changes in buying patterns and preferences also occur with a change in demographics. As your customers continue to age and you begin to receive younger clients, their preferences may be drastically different than their predecessors.

This has already happened in in U.S. over the past few decades. The millennial generation is much more cautious and much less enthusiastic while buying vehicles than were baby boomers. These types of changes will continue to occur, so the real question is, are you one step ahead of these changes?

The only way you can be a step ahead is to be constantly in touch with the customers. Constant contact with customers should form an unbroken chain of feedback. Imagine what you can do with years of data. You'll be able to see right through each and every step and strategy, and you'll be able to see it all through the customers' eyes. You'll be able to see exactly what's wrong and which areas require improvement. When you understand your customers, when you truly delve into their mindset, it's easier to impress them—even before they set foot in the dealership.

To do that, to know each and every aspect of the customers' preferences, you must receive their feedback on everything. This feedback should not be limited to how you greet or demonstrate. It should encompass all areas of activity—how you follow up with customers, the general attitude of the sales team, the quality of the products and the overall customer experience. It should even include information on the dealership itself in terms of how far it is from the customers and how clean it is. This is the level of detail required to truly know the customers inside and out, and that's part of your job if you want to sell thirty cars per month.

Customers can be a great resource when you're trying to identify problems, but what about when you're creating solutions? Would it surprise you to learn that the answer is the same? The customers are your ultimate resource. Granted, most of your customers won't know a single thing about conducting sales. They may have no expertise whatsoever in advising you on *how* to conduct business. In fact, their advice may sometimes seem counterproductive, and I'm not suggesting that you implement each and every one of their suggestions. All you need to do is to be on the lookout for *valuable* suggestions and, I assure you, every once in a while you'll hear something that will blow your mind. In fact, it will happen more often than you might expect.

Customers are smart and perceptive. They can often see the process from the outside much more clearly than you can from the inside. Oftentimes, the beauty of their suggestions lies in their simplicity. It's astounding to realize that, in your search to find sophisticated solutions, you may have overlooked such a simple detail, and that's the moment when you truly realize the value of customer feedback.

One of the keys to my success is that I have always valued my customers' suggestions. No matter how trivial or counterproductive a suggestion may seem, I always give it a fair bit of thought. On one hand, you have a single brain working infuriatingly hard to come up with solutions. On the other hand, you have hundreds—possibly thousands—of brains coming up with a solution almost effortlessly.

THE ADVANTAGES OF KNOWING YOUR NUMBERS

Let's be honest; I'm not the first person advising up-and-coming salespeople to know their numbers and do the math, nor will I be the last. Many of the so-called sales experts who have never once set foot on the sales floor offer the same advice. However, not many share the rationale behind their advice. Not many will tell you *why* you need to know your numbers. In order to do that, they would need considerable experience in sales, which is something many salespeople woefully lack.

In my years of experience, I learned the value of knowing your numbers and doing the math the hard way. I learned it through making mistakes, through trial and error. It wasn't easy, but as I incorporated these practices into my own sales process, I saw my sales numbers grow exponentially. I was only able to harness the power of numbers to my advantage when I was able to understand their advantages. If you want to be a successful salesperson, if you want to sell thirty cars per month, you must understand and implement these advantages to your benefit. Here are some of the advantages:

KNOW WHERE YOU STAND

In sales, success requires a degree of self-awareness. You need to be able to constantly measure your performance in order to know how close to or far from your goal you are at any given moment. What makes you a "good" salesperson? Is it merely a reflection of someone's subjective opinion? Not at all. It's an objective measure of your sales performance through numbers and sales figures. To put it simply, a good car salesperson is one who sells the most cars.

That said, daily or monthly car sales numbers are only the tip of the iceberg. A cursory glance at these numbers can show anyone the general state of sales performance, but that isn't what you're looking for. If you already know exactly where you stand, your sales numbers will tell you why you stand there. For instance, if your daily sales targets are nowhere near where you want them to be, you can refer to numbers such as the conversion ratio and qualitative data from customers to determine what aspect of your approach is not working.

DETERMINE WHERE YOU NEED TO GO

The other incredibly important function of these numbers is that they provide you with a sense of purpose and a direction in which you need to push yourself. For instance, if you're selling ten cars per month and you need to reach the thirty-car milestone, you don't want to aimlessly wander toward that goal. You must have a specific purpose; if you need to sell thirty cars per month, you need to triple your actions.

You also need to know which areas require the most effort, and that's where the numbers again come into play. If you have a reliable source of data, you'll know what your weakness is as a salesperson, and knowing in which areas you need to improve will give you the specific direction to take yourself.

UNDERSTAND THE INCENTIVE REQUIRED TO PUSH YOURSELF

Consider this: you have two sets of sales teams. The first has no sales targets and no incentives linked to those targets. The second is required to sell a given number of cars in a month. And, if they do so, they'll receive a hefty set of bonuses. Which team do you think will sell the most cars by the end of the month? Obviously the latter.

There's a reason that companies that focus on key performance indicators (KPIs) are much more productive than those that don't. When sales staff has set targets and incentives linked to achieving those targets, they go out of their way to perform well.

This is why knowing the numbers is extremely important. Knowing where you stand and where you need to go provides a clear distinction between expectations and eventual reality. Increasing your actions to achieve those numbers is most effective when it's linked to specific incentives. These incentives may be personal (such as a sense of achievement), or they may be monetary (such as doubling your salary or reaching the next bonus). Whatever the case may be, you will push yourself harder when you understand and follow the numbers.

MAINTAIN A HEALTHY BALANCE

I began this step by clarifying that car sales is a numbers game, and I stand by that statement. However, there's a catch. If forsaking the numbers while pointlessly meandering is one extreme, reducing sales down to mere numbers is another, and this is where many salespeople falter or outright fail. They invest all of their efforts in chasing numbers and forget about the customers, which is highly counterproductive. By overly obsessing with numbers, you will indirectly ensure that those numbers fall. Even if the numbers rise through shady sales practices, they won't be good in the long run.

The most important aspect of sales is pleasing the customer, and you must strike a balance between pleasing the customer and increasing sales numbers. Believe me, it's not hard, and the former leads to the latter. Invest honest efforts into it, and you'll come up with a mutually advantageous solution for you and your customers. Many businesses have faltered because they pushed their sales team too hard to achieve the numbers without caring about the needs of their customers. As a result, they ended up antagonizing their prospects and turning them away.

When you go for that number-centric approach, make sure that you make customer satisfaction an integral component of your statistical arsenal. Create a customer satisfaction index. Measure the happiness of your customers through their feedback. Regularly ask them to rate your services. Focus on creating loyal customers, and you'll see a direct correlation between your efforts and your sales numbers.

Closing the Deal

* * *

When you refer to a car sale, what you are actually referring to is the closing of the deal. It wouldn't be too off the mark to suggest that sales is, at its most basic level, only about closing the deal. If we ignore all the tips and techniques for effective sales for a moment and strip sales down to its core goal, what we are left with is the closing.

There's little point in knowing a lot about the product, demonstrating well and impressing the customer with your salesmanship skills if you cannot bring the customer to close the deal. At the end of the day, judging on the basis of numbers alone, your salesmanship skills are only gauged by the number of deals you are able to successfully close. Even the target of selling thirty cars per month is all about closing. No matter what else you do or how you do it, you need to close thirty deals in the month. Better salesmanship only brings you closer to the target. You have to reach up and grab it using the skills required to close the deal.

If you take Alec Baldwin's advice in *Glengarry Glen Ross* to heart, all you need to do is ABC: "Always Be Closing. Always Be Closing. *Always Be Closing!*" As an ambitious salesperson, that's what you aspire to. That's what you live for. There's nothing more important to you than closing the deal. Arm yourself with the art of closing the deal. Learn the skills it takes to close well. Train yourself; rehearse common closing techniques often. Gain valuable experience, and avoid common mistakes.

The word "closing" is casually thrown around. Close the deal, close the sale, close the customer. As salespeople, we hear it often. But *how* we close exactly? And what does it even mean when we say close? Usually, when a word is thrown around so casually and used in so many different contexts, it loses its original meaning.

In simple terms, closing can be defined as an action through which you transform a prospective buyer into a customer. It's the last step of any financial transaction. Although your sales process may continue on even after you close the deal, the actual "sale" of the product is completed when the deal is closed. It's the point at which when you hand over ownership of the product to the customer in exchange for money or the promise of money. In car sales, closing is when you sign the contract after agreeing to mutually discussed terms and conditions.

However, it's not always successful. From the moment the customer walks in to the dealership (and even before), until the customer sits around the table to discuss the terms, there's a lot that can go wrong. Closing the deal is, therefore, inextricably linked to every other step in the process. It is the product of your earlier efforts and cannot function independently. Anything that goes wrong in the earlier steps of the sales process can sabotage the closing, so when you focus on closing, you need to focus on the earlier steps as well.

When it comes to learning the art of closing the deal, you need to avoid two of the common mistakes committed by salespeople who are just starting out.

One mistake is considering the closing as the Holy Grail. These salespeople focus a significant portion of their energy and learning experience on how to close the deal without paying much heed to the preliminary steps. They may enjoy limited success in the beginning and may see their sales numbers rise dramatically. However, such success is highly unstable and usually short-lived. Closing the deal without providing a valuable customer experience causes disillusionment among the customers, and they choose to learn from their mistakes and not buy from that dealership again.

The other mistake is made by those for whom the idea of sales consists mostly of demonstrating the vehicle and impressing the customers with their knowledge of the products. They focus more on heavily rehearsed speeches than actual conversations. They may be good orators, but they are not good communicators. And, yes, there's a difference. Sales is a two-way process in which you need to interact with a customer, engaging in a back-and-forth discussion rather than simply trying to convince him to buy. It's frustrating to be part of this group since they consistently find it difficult to close the deal at the end of the day.

To be a successful closer, you need to find the critical balance between these two groups. You need to understand that, although other steps in the sales process are critical to bringing the customer to the closing table, it takes an exceptional amount of skill to *keep* them there and get them to sign on the dotted line. You need to be careful while exercising the skill. Closing the deal is not the only thing that matters. The way in which you do it matters equally. If you do it well, it may be considered an artful closing. If not, it's potentially conning the customer. It’s your job to maintain that steady balance and not merely close but close with consideration for the customers' needs

Therefore, a close analysis of closing in car sales reveals that it is one of the most significant steps—not simply because it's the step in which you exchange the product for money, but also because it's the natural end point of all earlier steps and the starting point of all later ones. A successful closing also depends upon a variety of factors including, but not limited to, how well you greet a customer, how well you present and demonstrate and how personable and charming you are. However, almost as important as these factors, if not more so, is the ability to get the customer to sign.

In addition to knowing *how* to close, it’s also significant that you know *when* to close. Just like everything else, this requires skill and balance. You need to avoid the mistakes others commit. In this area, too, there are two kinds of salespeople you don’t want to be. There are those who go in for the close too early and others who do so too late. You need to be skilled at not only finding the best way to convince the customers but also finding that brief window—that golden opportunity—to finally pose the big question.

Timing is critical, and the right timing depends on the nature of your relationship and the level of communication with the customer. The former dictates whether the customer feels comfortable enough with you to agree to the sale earlier on than usual. The latter determines whether or not you can accurately assess whether the customer is willing to buy at any given time.

The traditional view of closing is nearly obsolete, and we're moving toward a new definition of the concept. Closing is no longer simply a numbers game. It's an experience wherein two human beings interact in order to create a financial and commercial relationship. It's hard to illustrate this transformation through words alone but Jeff Thull, author of *Mastering The Complex Sale*, has managed to do it well. He says:

In the rush to close deals, we too often forget the human factor and squander the long-term opportunity. We need to address the hopes, fears, and aspirations of our customers and create mutually beneficial relationships.

Pay attention to Thull's keywords: hopes, fears, aspirations and mutually beneficial relationships. These are profoundly human terms. Note that he does not talk about the technical aspects of how and when to close. Instead he chooses to capture the human spirit that lies *behind* the physical actions involved in closing the deal. The technical details can come later, but we must first understand what it takes to adapt to this new approach—the key human emotions we need to consider in lieu of crude numbers alone. By focusing on, and understanding, the essence of the thought that lies behind the actions, we can develop the ability to close well and more often.

Let's now put this new approach into its new context by comparing it with the old one. The traditional view of closing the deal was extremely simple. I prefer the term "simplistic." That view held that every person interested in buying a vehicle is a prospect, and every prospect has cash in his pocket and an urge to buy the product in his heart. The businessman has the product to sell, and the salesperson is the one who has the incentive to carry out the financial transaction. It is his job to sell as many products as possible and to bring in as much money as possible. Sales was, for a time, reduced to a game of numbers, and the job of the salesperson was to score the most numbers by closing the most deals.

That was the old formula, and the old formula is obsolete. It doesn't work anymore. More and more businesspeople and salespersons are beginning to recognize and reject the old formula. More and more organizations are moving away from the traditionalist approach. There are various reasons why we need such a shift and how it can be beneficial for businesses in the long run.

Plain and simple, customers' expectations have changed over the years. When you sell for the sake of money and not for the sake of customers, those customers believe that they have been shortchanged. They simply don't buy from the same company again when there are so many alternative options that provide much better service. Therefore, good customer care is not simply a matter of positive morality. It's a business necessity. If your business doesn't get repeat clients, there will come a time when you will no longer have a business. It's that simple.

Aside from business considerations, other factors are also critical. Today's customers are smart, perceptive and highly observant. We don't do them any favors by giving them the attention they require. They deserve each and every bit of our care. They deserve to be treated as human beings instead of sales targets and, if they aren't, they'll simply turn elsewhere. One quick Google search can change everything you've worked so hard for, and when you have to compete with the entire digital landscape instead of merely your direct competition, it goes without saying that you need to up your game.

Common Closing Techniques

Like many other sales techniques, common closing techniques are a valuable addition to your arsenal. And, like other techniques, these are not one-size-fits-all solutions that can be applied on any and every customer. More than the technique itself, it's important to have the skills and presence of mind to be able to choose the right technique for the right customer at the right time. A technique is not a shortcut or a trick. It's a way to channel your inner skills. You can't yield results simply by applying a random technique in a random situation. Techniques provide you with a way to work smart rather than hard, but you need to put in work all the same to get the desired end result.

Some common closing techniques:

OPINION CLOSE

Sometimes, the best approach to closing a deal is also the simplest. All you need to do is ask the customer whether or not he wants to close and, if not, why. Simple enough, right? The opinion close may be simple, but that doesn't make it any less effective. In fact, you may be surprised at the kinds of results a simple yes or no question can yield.

Suppose you demonstrate a vehicle to the customer and he appears impressed. Something holds him back, however, from making that final decision and giving you the final "Yes." You know there's something wrong. You can sense it. You can even see it on his face. What do you do?

Honestly, it doesn't hurt to simply ask!

In a way, the opinion close shows your honesty, straightforwardness and no-nonsense attitude to sales. But you shouldn't overdo it; remember to be polite to the customer. Don't appear overly inquisitive. You can ask about his concerns in a friendly and reassuring way, but ask nonetheless. Your goal, in an opinion close, is to engage in a conversation with the customer. What is it that's stopping him from making a deal? Is it the price? Something else? These seemingly simple straightforward questions, when asked politely, can make a huge difference and yield surprising results.

ASSUMPTIVE CLOSE

This is a technique to be used when you're confident about the customer's position. Suppose you're certain that the process has gone well to this point, and you're receiving positive signals from the customer. You know that there's no way that the customer will say "No." At this point, it's time to make a move. When you go for the assumptive close, don't ask. Don't suggest. Simply assume that all will work out for the best and that the next logical step is to close the deal. Present the customer with the document, a pen and no questions. Usually, the customer happily obliges.

The assumptive close is the confident approach to selling. It works best in situations when you are absolutely certain that the customer will buy. It can also work well with customers who want to buy but are slightly nervous about the deal. In such a situation, your confidence will be a source of reassurance for the customers.

When attempting the assumptive close, it's best to cut to the chase straight away. You don't need to appear too overbearing, however. Make the request for the close seem like a question or a suggestion. If you cannot say, "Here, sign on the dotted line," you can say something like, "How would you like to pay?" or "Let's move on to your loan application."

NOW-OR-NEVER CLOSE

Sometimes it helps to put slight pressure on the customer. It's the final straw that breaks the proverbial camel's back, the final push that forces the customer over the edge. It's important to note that I'm not asking you to force the customer to make a decision when he doesn't want to. That goes against everything we have discussed until this point. This technique only serves to quicken the decision for those who are indecisive by nature. It provides an incentive to the customer to make the right decision—and soon.

The now-or-never close allows you to use time to your advantage in order to put pressure on the customer. You provide the customer with a brief window of opportunity in which to make the final decision. It's now or never, short notice, no delay. You make a special offer to the customer, an offer that is attractive but limited by time. For instance, "If you sign today, you can receive a two percent discount." Notice that there are two elements of the offer: time sensitivity and reward. These two components of your offer must both be present.

BALANCE SHEET CLOSE

One of the customer types we discussed in the previous chapter under the DECS mechanism was the Stable/Analytical customer. The best way to manage this type of customer is to adopt an analytical and systematic approach to closing by combining the analytical and systematic elements of the DECS mechanism. Apply a visual aesthetic to the proceeding, and you will have a balance-sheet close. In this scenario you get to learn from none other than Benjamin Franklin himself:

> *"My way is to divide half a sheet of paper by a line into two columns, writing over the one Pro and over the other Con."*

Grab a piece of paper and pen, and get ready to convince your customer with a combination of logic and visuals. Before you do that, however, ask yourself this question: "Why exactly do I need to do that? What exactly is my goal?" Your goal, obviously, is to convince the customer to purchase. Therefore, your entire approach to the balance sheet will be to create a visual map that helps convince him that the decision he's making is the right one. Don't get too bogged down in technical details. Make sure to create a long and healthy Pros column and a short Cons column. If you do everything right, the deal is likely in your pocket.

SUMMARY CLOSE

The summary close is similar to the balance-sheet close in that it's analytical and systematic. Unlike the balance sheet approach, however, it is oral rather than visual. When you go for a summary close, you present a detailed account of all of the advantages of buying the product and all the details you've covered up to that point.

Repeating the experience can be an effective tool for the customer as it creates an aura of familiarity, a feeling that he has been a part of an experience *with* you. It helps build trust with the customer, and this feeling of mutual trust is one that you can build upon later to reiterate to the customer all the positive aspects of the vehicle. When you do that *after* you've created a bond with the customer, he is more likely to have confidence in you than he was earlier.

APOLOGY CLOSE

One of the most sincere things you can do as a salesperson is apologize, and a sincere apology can take you a long way. This is what you will discover when you attempt the apology close. As the name suggests, what you do is apologize. You take the blame of the potentially failing deal upon yourself.

The key is to take the customer by surprise. Begin with, "I'm sorry. I owe you an apology." Now you have his attention. "Why is he apologizing?" he wonders. Some even wonder this aloud!

"I must have skipped out on some crucial information somewhere along the way," you explain. "I'm sorry I couldn't be a better salesperson."

If forming a connection with the customer is your goal, the connection you form after a sincere apology is the purest. You cannot believe how well this technique works when applied in certain situations. It's genuinely surprising to many of the customers and catches them utterly off-guard. You can, then, use their surprise to your advantage. The opinion close is an effective way to begin negotiations again—even after they have seemingly reached a point of no return. You use the apology as a springboard from which to launch into a conversation about what exactly went wrong. Once you're in it, you win it.

Top 10 Closing Mistakes

Just as salesmanship involves following tried-and-true techniques and avoiding common mistakes, there are also a number of don'ts involved in closing the deal. I've seen many experienced salespeople commit some of these basic mistakes and lose valuable business. If your goal is to sell thirty cars per month, you cannot afford to make any of these mistakes.

CLOSING TOO SOON

In our earlier discussions about closing, we discovered that knowing *when* to close is as important as knowing *how* to close. Good salespersons have the ability to easily find that Goldilocks time zone—one that is neither too hot nor too cold. If you want to close more deals, you need to know what that time is.

If you try to close before the customer is ready, two things might happen. The customer might think you're a pushy salesperson trying to force him to buy a product. Or, the customer might mistrust you—after all, there must surely be something wrong with the product if you want to sell it so badly. You don't want either of these scenarios to occur, so wait. Take a deep breath. Let the customer make up his own mind and, if possible, assist him in that process. Close only when you're quite sure you'll get a "Yes."

WAITING TOO LONG

I've seen many experienced salespersons commit this mistake. When you're new, all you care about is impressing the customer. But as you learn more and gain more valuable experience, you come to know that there are other (more important) tasks to accomplish as well.

One of those tasks is closing the deal. You must know when to stop impressing the customers and start trying to yield the results of your efforts by closing the deal. In every customer-salesperson conversation, there's a natural time to close. If you continue to talk past that point, you can easily dissuade the customer from buying the product.

FAILING TO NOTICE THE CLOSE

The aforementioned mistakes can be easily avoided if you notice the exact perfect time to close. As a sales manager, it's frustrating to see how many salespersons fail to notice the close, even though it's right there in front of him. The customer is clearly ready to buy. He's willing to give you his money. Are you willing to take it?

This is why I stress the importance of a two-way conversation between the customer and the salesperson. Open yourself up to pick up on the cues that suggest that the customer is willing to close the deal. Be perceptive and observant. Look for visible signals. If the customer looks visibly happy and impressed, it is time to close the deal.

IGNORING THE INFLUENCERS

In our earlier discussions, we talked about the impact influencers can have. An influencer is the person who, even without the power to make the final decision, can wield considerable influence over the key decision maker. Influencers are an integral part of your target audience. It is necessary that you direct your sales pitch to them as well, and it's a crime not to include them in the closing process.

This step becomes particularly crucial when the decision maker is unwilling to listen to what you have to say. In this scenario, the influencer can be incredibly useful in terms of exercising his authority to get the decision maker to a decision point. You need to win the influencer's trust in order to close the deal.

DEPENDING TOO HEAVILY ON THE DEMONSTRATION

Let's face it—buying a car is not an easy decision. It's not like buying groceries, which you do almost impulsively. Not only is it much more expensive, it has a longer-term impact. When you buy a car, you have to live with it for a long time, so it's natural that the customer will want some time to deliberate no matter how great the car may be.

Your job as a salesperson is not only to demonstrate how technically brilliant the product is. Many customers can easily discover that over the Internet. You are there to assist the customer in making the decision he *wants* to make. If you rely too heavily on the presentation and not at all on the closing, you're not doing your job properly.

BEING A MECHANICAL SALES MACHINE

The best way you can assist the customer in making hard decisions is to be human. If you want to sell thirty cars per month, you need to learn how to cultivate a relationship with your customers. There's no alternative to that; you must understand the customer's emotions and discover how best to influence them. That is the trick to closing the deal.

Tact and wit can only take you so far. What makes a salesperson truly brilliant is emotional intelligence. This form of intelligence is what will enable you to close far more deals than usual. Instead of merely restating facts that anyone can easily access, let's work to make buying a better experience for the customer.

IGNORING WHAT THE CUSTOMER WANTS

I've been a salesperson for decades now, and I absolutely understand the pressures of sales targets. I understand how desperately you want to sell a particular number of vehicles per month. I also understand that you need to do your best to sell *specific* vehicles. However, if you attempt to focus on those two targets more than the wishes of your customers, you'll end up neither satisfying the customers nor making the required number of sales.

The best way to proceed is to do your best to understand *exactly* what the customer wants and deliver precisely that. This is the only way you can close fast and close more often. When you receive and close more customers, you have both the chance of meeting your monthly sales numbers and selling more of the assigned vehicles.

RELYING ON REHEARSED SALES PITCHES

This is an approach you can perhaps get away with in the demonstration phase but *absolutely not* when it comes time to close the deal. This is an area that distinguishes good salespersons from bad. Whereas the demonstration is a one-way flow of information, the closing is more of a balanced two-way conversation between the customer and the salesperson. There's nothing more painful than to watch a salesperson continue on with his well-rehearsed messages.

Customers are smart. They can easily tell what's going on even when you cannot. It's like a comedian who begins to perform his rehearsed stand-up material in the middle of a normal conversation. You instantly notice it! Stay as far away from a rehearsed or fake-sounding sales pitch as possible. Instead, let the conversation blossom organically. Even if you are practicing some of the previously discussed closing techniques, never let the customer know that you're using a tried-and-true method of selling. If all else fails, throw everything out of the window and try to sell to them as a person, not a sales target.

BEING NEGATIVE

A good sales experience is one that makes the customer happy, not brings him down. It's up to you to find a way to sell the product in a way that overflows with positive energy and stays as far away from negativity as possible. If you're trying to set your products or promotions apart from your competition, say that they are the best in the market. Don't say that some of the other products and services are not up to par. Don't contaminate the conversation with negativity. When you avoid attacking your competitors, it makes you appear more truthful, trustworthy and sincere.

This advice is also particularly relevant if you're offering a discount or making any other offer. There are two ways to offer discounts. The first is, "If you buy this now, you will get a two percent discount." The second is, "If you don't buy this now, you won't get a two percent discount." Although it's the same offer, the former approach is clearly the better one. Customers don't like being told what they *cannot* do.

BEING OVERLY AGGRESSIVE

This advice is particularly relevant when you're trying to attempt the now-or-never close. Although the now-or-never technique is predicated on putting slight pressure on the customer by giving him a time limit, it does *not* give you the right to overly pressure the customer. Even if you bully him to the point of buying your product, he certainly won't return to your dealership, and we've discussed at length why that is a problem.

The overly aggressive sales model is obsolete. Simply focus on the expectations of the customers. When the customer enters your dealership, he expects to be treated with care and respect. He doesn't want to be harassed or bullied. If you won't meet his expectations, there are plenty of other dealerships available to him.

The Follow-Up

* * *

In some ways, the follow-up is the most underrated and underused component of the sales process. Consequently, it can become your secret weapon to boost sales. And what a weapon it is! I've seen many organizations and salespeople double—even triple—their sales figures by maintaining a good follow-up strategy. It's an exceptional way to create a firm repeat client base and generate referral business. Additionally, if done well it allows you to significantly enhance your customer satisfaction ratings. That, too, can feed into repeats client and referral streams. It's a multipurpose tool that, if wielded effectively, can work wonders for you in the long run.

Before we explore the advantages of a great follow-up in detail, it is essential to learn what following up with the customers actually means. By definition, to follow up means to keep in touch with existing customers after the sale or with prospects after the first visit to your dealership. They are equally important in your quest to sell thirty cars per month. Although we consider both of these follow-ups part of one big approach, there are many differences and other factors to consider, some of which we will discuss in detail.

However, behind all of this effort lies a sole purpose: to drastically increase the number of sales and boost your customer satisfaction ratio. To be successful, you need a systematic approach to following up with clients and prospects. Organization is one of the most important requirements of a good follow-up. A strong follow-up requires specific skills, a staggering amount of patience and an almost magical ability to instantly connect with people. You need to have all that. Above all, you need to have an organized effort, a system with individual components that work together to perform a much larger function.

When you perform that function well, several things happen. With a great follow-up, you can transform prospects into clients and one-time customers into long-time customers. One of the most difficult aspects of selling thirty cars per month is maintaining a steady stream of walk-in clients who are ready to buy your products. Many dealerships don't have that. Therefore, the only way you can ensure that there are enough customers willing to buy your products is to maintain a continuous practice of following up with clients and prospects.

There are many businesses that do not realize this simple fact. They either ignore the follow-up entirely or do not put great effort into it. Even by most optimistic estimates, without a good follow-up, sales numbers remain stagnant, no closer to their target of thirty cars per month per salesperson. What usually happens is, sales numbers begin a downward trajectory and do not come back. This is what you need to avoid at all costs.

Although there are many ways through which to utilize your follow-up skills, two are the most relevant when it comes to boosting monthly car sales: following up with sold customers and following up with unsold prospects.

Both of these follow-ups require entirely different approaches and mindset and yield entirely different results. The circumstances of the interactions may be different, but the ultimate goal is the same: sell thirty cars per month.

What do you think when a potential customer steps into your dealership? Most salespersons in your place think, “Great! I’ll make another sale today.” While it’s an admirable sentiment, it’s not the one that yields the best results. The next time a customer walks into the dealership, don’t think about the immediate prospect of the sale. Think about the opportunity to forge a relationship.

Just that thought alone can have a huge impact on the way you engage with the customer. If you engage with him simply to sell a vehicle, that’s well and good, and the customer may or may not come back. But when you engage the customer with the sole purpose of creating a relationship, all your actions lead toward that—not to mention the fact that you may also make the sale!

The next logical step, then, is the follow-up. Many salespeople believe that the follow-up is simply following up with a prospective buyer. And indeed, that seems to be the case in most kinds of sales. Car sales, however, are fundamentally different. On average, Americans buys five or six cars in their lifetime. Wit that in mind, why are you content with simply selling a customer one car? You need to think big; not only is your goal to bring the customer back again, but you also need to think about gaining referrals, which can be the backbone of any business endeavor. Every customer is a goldmine of contacts, and the leads they each send you are not acquired from a random list of prospects. They're solid hot prospective buyers who enter your dealership on a recommendation from someone they trust.

HOW TO EFFECTIVELY FOLLOW UP WITH CUSTOMERS

FOLLOWING UP WITH SOLD PROSPECTS

Call the customer immediately after the sale

Once you've established the relationship, don't let it cool off. Strike when it's hot. The best way to do that is to call the customer immediately after the sale. Doing that sends a strong message that, even though you got the sale, you still care about the customer.

Call the customer two weeks after the sale

There's not much point in asking the customer about his experience with the vehicle immediately after he purchases it, but two weeks after the sale is a good time to ask. Also, you can ask the customer to rate you on the service you provided him.

Call the customer a month after the sale

In the first two follow-ups, you established a steady relationship with the customer. Now it's time to go for the big request. Ask him if they would like to refer your dealership to anyone he knows.

Keep in touch periodically

Once you've gotten what you wanted and needed from the customer, it's time to forget him and move on, right? *Wrong!* You should still keep in touch—if only so that the customer doesn't forget that you exist. A good way to do that is by sending regular birthday or holiday greetings and making personalized phone calls.

FOLLOWING UP WITH UNSOLD PROSPECTS

Although following up with unsold customers is a staple of sales, there are many car dealerships that do not utilize this immensely beneficial opportunity. Those with the traditional view of car sales wait for the customers to walk into the dealership on their own. This sales model has worked for many dealerships—until now. Why change? There are many reasons.

Selling thirty cars per month is not an easy task to begin with, and most dealerships do not receive enough customers to be able to do it. Therefore, your first task is to increase the amount of walk-in traffic. Although your existing customers are a valuable source for referral traffic, it's not enough to rely on them entirely. You need to look elsewhere.

Any experienced salesperson will tell you that calling prospects only once is not enough. Persistence and repetition are the keys to a successful approach to contacting prospects. You need to repeat your message again and again until it sinks in. Sales research suggests that it takes five calls or more to convince a huge majority of prospects, and I'm sure the majority of salespersons quit after the third call. Only those who persist take the lion's share of prospects.

Don't ignore the "just looking" customers

Let's face it. One of the trickiest situations you can be in as a salesperson is dealing with customers who seem to be "just looking." Some salespeople choose to ignore them entirely, and they couldn't be more wrong in their approach. The "just looking" customers are one of the best leads you can procure. Most of them want to buy a vehicle at some point—probably when they can better afford it. It's a guaranteed sale opportunity. Would you let it go so easily?

One of the first things you must do with these customers is note their details. Take their name and number. Additionally, you need to ascertain some of their personal preferences such as the vehicle they want to buy and the price they can afford. After they've left, stay in touch. Many of the "just looking" customers do not expect to receive great customer service, and this is your chance to surprise them.

Keep in touch with the prospects

The key to successful follow-up with unsold prospects is not to break a constant chain of communication. Whether it's a greeting card or a follow-up email, you need to keep reminding them of your existence.

Ask for referrals

Why should your sold customers be your only source for referrals? Your prospects are equally capable of bringing as many prospective clients as your sold customers, so always ask them for a referral. Even if they're not yet ready to buy a vehicle, someone they know might be.

5 Secrets to Mastering Sales Follow-Ups

* * *

In his book *No B.S. Ruthless Management of People and Profits*, Dan S. Kennedy presents five ways you can significantly improve your follow-up game. These are the five steps that you can apply on the general follow-up process to yield results.

His five principles helped my team and me not only to close more sales from our leads, it also significantly reduced the time it took to make a sale. Let us examine these five secrets and how you can employ them in selling thirty cars per month.

UNDERSTAND LEAD TYPES

Kennedy describes three kinds of leads you can work on in your follow-up phase. These are:

Hot

These are among the most valuable leads you can be offered. Hot leads are the ones you can sell to right away. Among them are people looking for cars and ready to buy at that moment. You don't need to work hard on these leads; simply say the right thing and the sale is in your pocket.

Warm

Warm leads are ones who *may* buy a car in the near future. Since the hot leads don't require a lot of attention on your part, you'll work harder on warm leads than hot leads. Warm leads are the ones you deal with the most since the hot ones are rare and/or already buying. Second, whether or not warm leads buy from you depends upon the nature of follow-up, and it must be so good that they cannot resist.

Cold

You may guess by the name that these are the leads who may not buy a vehicle in their lifetime. Some call them dead leads and prefer to leave them on their own, but a smart salesperson will find a way to do something with even the coldest of leads. One day, they might just turn warm.

ENSURE PERFECT TIMING

The essence of the perfect follow-up, if expressed in a single word, is timing. Correct timing can make all the difference in the world. You have to perform all the tasks on the timeline that best suits the customer. He will buy when he's ready to buy. To ensure perfect timing, you need three basic elements:

Team

You need a dedicated team of individuals to assist you in the follow-up process. They can belong to the marketing, telecommunication or IT department. Successful follow-up requires a collective effort.

System

Once you have a team of great salespeople ready to their job, they need a system to follow. It's your job to come up with that.

Tools

Once you have the team and the system, the only thing missing is a set of proper tools that the team can use to implement the system. Once those tools have been acquired, the essential prerequisites for a follow-up are in hand.

INTEGRATE SALES AND MARKETING

Kennedy bases his advice around the sales model where the bulk of sales is conducted over the phone. That isn't the case with car sales, so we must interpret his advice a bit differently. In order to carry out an effective follow-up, you need to be a salesperson and a marketer at the same time.

In business organizations, salespeople are usually asked to sell the actual product while the marketer's job is to follow up with the prospects. In car sales, we have no such distinction. You are the salesperson *and* the marketer. It is your job both to sell the product and perform the follow-up. And since you know the customer the best, you are the perfect person for the job.

MAINTAIN A LIVING, BREATHING DATABASE

We have discussed the importance of the right tools and the right system to ensure perfect follow-up. One of the most valuable of those tools is a customer database. What exactly does the database consist of? What comes to your mind when you think of the database? For many salespeople, a database contains a list of customer names and contact numbers. It's similar to a list of leads. This is not, however, even close to the type of database I have in mind. If you want to perfect your follow-up game, you need to operate with more than a simple list of names and numbers.

The type of list I have in mind contains not only the clients' and prospects' contact details but also a separate profile for each contact. In this file, you save all details of the previous financial transactions with the customers including all products they've purchased and their billing information. You must take copious notes for each prospect or customer, including personal details such as date of birth, details from the previous follow-up and the next scheduled appointment. The more information you have, the more successful you will be in creating relationships with your customers.

I considered all this and more when I set out to design the database I mentioned earlier, The Autominer (http://www.theautominer.com). My two main goals were simplifying target marketing and increasing customer retention. I spent an enormous amount of time with the IT team perfecting the database, which now allows me to:

- Perform a quick and timely search for the right customers
- Filter search results on the basis of client or date
- Print, send and export emails and messages
- Create customer lists
- Create work plans
- Schedule, track and perform calls
- And much, much more

EDUCATION, REPETITION AND VARIETY

According to Kennedy, a perfect follow-up approach must be a combination of the following three elements:

Education

Forget for a moment that you are a salesperson, and place yourself in the customer's shoes. If you were a customer, how would like a perfect follow-up to be executed? Surely you wouldn't have wanted to spend your valuable time interacting with a salesperson but getting nothing in return. This is what you need to consider when formulating a follow-up. A perfect follow-up does its job, but it does so while providing value to the customer.

Repetition

The average human attention span has now been reduced to 6-8 seconds. Think about that for a moment. Even if you carefully craft a sales message and find creative ways to deliver it, chances are you won't be able to engage the customer for more than eight seconds. This is why repetition is important. It's the same technique advertisers use. We hear the message again and again and again until it finally sinks in. If you want your customers to remember you, find ways to contact them again and again and again without being too overbearing or pushy. Space out your messages enough that prospects feel comfortable receiving them, but don't space them out so far that they forget about you in the interim and purchase somewhere else. Repetition is the key, but there must be innovation in repetition. Your messages must be engaging and fun, not boring or tedious.

Variety

The follow-up must be varied. Use different kinds of media to your advantage. You have mail, email, phone, fax and social media at your disposal. There are so many options to reach potential customers. Use all of these means when creating an effective follow-up strategy.

10 Successful Follow-Up Techniques

* * *

Once you perfect the five secrets to playing the follow-up game, you can move on to specific follow-up techniques that may help to ensure an effective follow-up.

SELECT THE BEST MEDIUM

This principle sounds simple enough. You must choose the best medium to reach your potential customer. You cannot rely on testing random mediums and seeing which one works best—that's the equivalent of throwing a bunch of darts at the board to see which (if any) sticks.

Each of the mediums for follow-up has its own uses and is suitable for a particular class of customers. It's your job to select which medium is best for which message and customer. The nature of your follow-up message and your target audience are different depending on the medium you choose. For instance, phones are best for a more personalized conversation. Emails, on the other hand, are perfect for one-way communications. And social media is the right avenue for an engaging experience. Each medium has specific applications.

CREATIVELY CRAFT YOUR MESSAGE

When it comes to follow-up, what you say is as important as how often you choose to say it. Before you pick up that phone or type that email, consider what your message can offer the customer. Is it informative? Is it meant to be engaging? Or, is it a boring generic message that you've sent to a thousand customers?

If it's the latter, you need to go back to the drawing board. It's not hard to create personalized follow-up messages for the customer. All you need is a database and enough information to work with. You can use humor in your follow-up messages; you can also choose to make them informative or interesting for the customers.

DON'T SIMPLY SAY YOU'RE "TOUCHING BASE"

If there's one practice I dislike the most in follow-up, it's the practice of saying, "Hey, I'm just calling to touch base." Is there any message more boring, generic or instantly forgettable? If you want to be successful in follow-up, stop using this phrase at once. Promise me!

Now that you have vowed never to use it again in a follow-up conversation, let's find some more creative ways to open a follow-up conversation. If you can't think of anything, ask the customer about his day. Or, refer to your last conversation and talk about a detail the customer mentioned in passing. Say anything but "I'm just touching base."

FIND A SPECIFIC REASON TO FOLLOW UP

One of the reasons why "touching base" messages don't work well is that it seems as though you're pestering the customer for no good reason. All you're doing is checking up or sending a generic message that you sent to a hundred different customers already. Even if you're doing both of those things, it's your job not to let the customer know that.

Instead, find specific reasons to follow up. You may be calling them to ask how their experience buying with you went, or to remind them to rate your dealership for customer service. Or, you may be calling to ask for referrals. All of these are examples of specific reasons to follow up.

ALWAYS PLAN AHEAD WITH THE CUSTOMER

Suppose you have a productive follow-up conversation with the customer. Where do you go from there? If you hang up without a future appointment or any other plan, you're digging yourself a deep hole. You're closing the doors for the future, and you cannot afford to do that.

This is why you always need to plan ahead with the customer. Always set up the next appointment or a milestone that you to achieve in your next conversation. Don't hang up the phone until you're able to receive a commitment from the customer.

The simplest way to do that is to ask the customer for their permission to call or contact him again. It's easy if you're nice enough. If the customer doesn't agree to a future call, you can ask to email him. Asking permission is a great way to establish a relationship of trust with the customer. This way, when you follow up, you aren't pestering; you're merely obliging.

MAINTAIN COPIOUS NOTES

If there's one piece of follow-up advice I always offer young salespeople, it's to maintain *a lot* of notes. Gather all the information you can about a customer. Record the calls, if you must, but only with their permission. Note down their birthdates and the time of the next appointment. Make notes about the number of calls you have made to the customer and what you discussed in each of those calls. There's a lot of potential information you can miss out on, but you can avoid all that by developing the habit of maintaining copious notes.

Why do you need to do that in the first place? The reason is simple. When you're contacting hundreds of people for a follow-up, you can't remember each and every detail that might be helpful for the next conversation. Keeping those notes handy not only helps you remember the customer's preferences, it also personalizes the future conversation. When you have all the information at hand, it's easier to impress customers with your memory.

CREATE A FOLLOW-UP SCHEDULE

This step combines the earlier two steps of maintaining notes and planning ahead. Before we dive in, let me reiterate that if you don't create a follow-up schedule, you're in deep trouble. You might as well not follow up at all. Following up without a schedule is like working on a cluttered desk. It's not fun, and everything takes longer than usual. You need to clear up the clutter and begin everything from scratch.

The first step is to acquire an empty calendar or planner. You can use a simple diary, or you can use a specialized follow-up program like TheAutominer.com. Fill out each calendar entry with any number of prospects that you want to call in a day. Evenly space out the time between two consecutive calls. For instance, repeat every entry after a month or every two months. When you fill up the calendar to the brim, it's time to pick up the phone and start calling. Once you engage actively in the follow-up process, you'll notice the calendar beginning to take shape somewhat organically.

You'll need to set up future appointments and move existing ones to a new date. Your schedule will be dynamic and organized. Your follow-ups will be successful.

BUILD A FOLLOW-UP CUSTOMER DATABASE

All of your notes and schedule entries belong in the customer database along with the bills and ledgers. You can choose to create two separate databases for existing customers and prospective buyers. Or, you can cram it all into a single database. Do whatever works the best for you. The fact of the matter is that you need a customer database in order to ensure successful follow-up in an organized manner. This can be your greatest asset when it comes to follow-up. If you don't have a database, you don't have the mechanism through which you can get organized, and you'll again be operating from a cluttered desk.

This is why I, along with my IT team and my good friend James DiMeo Jr., created The Autominer, my own data-mining tool. It makes it incredibly easy for me to note copious customer details, make appointments in an instant and keep sales records in one place. The Autominer made my life simpler and free from all the hassle and stress of follow-up.

CHOOSE THE PERFECT DAY/TIME TO MAKE THE CALL

Since timing is one of the most important considerations when it comes to successful follow-ups, we need to be careful in choosing the best time and days to make the follow-up call. Here, we can rely on statistical data, however there is nothing more important than what the customer wants.

Statistics show that Thursdays are the best time to call customers for follow-up. Not Tuesdays, not Fridays, but Thursdays. Data show that Tuesdays and Fridays are the worst days to call. There's also evidence that Sundays and other holidays might work, although I personally avoid those times.

When it comes to the time of day, research suggests that 4:00-6:00pm are the best times to call, as customers are expected to be more relaxed in post-business hours. The worst time to call is between 12:00-2:00pm. It's imperative to mention here that these are the days and times that generally work best in sales, but the most important criteria is what works best for the customer. If he wants you to call on Tuesday at 1:00 pm, that's when you call!

BE REPETITIVE BUT NOT PESKY

This is based on Shark Tank investor Kevin O'Leary's advice to "be sticky, not gummy." What does he mean when he says that? How can you be repetitive without being annoying? The key is to be mindful of what customers want. Set appointments in advance so that the next time you call, it's not a bother.

Whatever you do, don't call customers once and leave it at that. You need to be what I call "conveniently repetitive." But how much do you repeat yourself? That is the question. For best results, you need to call a prospect at least six times. According to some surveys, a staggering 93 percent of converted leads are reached on the sixth attempt. How many calls do *you* make to your prospects? It's something to think about.

Be Everywhere

* * *

We live in a world of constant noise. It's a world filled with a cacophony of distraction coming from everywhere at all times. Our goal is not just to survive in such a world but to thrive and succeed in it. You're not here simply to compete. You're here to dominate. To do that, you need to be everywhere. You need to capture every potential prospect's imagination in a unique or creative way. You need to grab the lion's share of the market for yourself, and that is only possible through a creatively designed strategy, some tried-and-true techniques and a whole lot of hard work.

Assuming that you're employing the 4-3-2-1 Rule discussed earlier, if you want to sell 30 vehicles by the end of the month, you need to receive at least 120 customers. This is a huge target, and you can only achieve that by being everywhere.

On the surface, it seems like simple advice: be everywhere. Increase your efforts by ten times. Reach the maximum number of customers you can. Use various media outlets, both traditional and digital, to spread your message everywhere. The goal is to drive traffic to your dealership. It sounds good, but when you get down to the specifics of how to do it, or when you attempt it in real life, that's when you realize how monumental of a task it is. You need to exhaust every available resource you have to achieve this one purpose. You have to spend a significant portion of your energy laying the groundwork that will allow you to sell more cars.

You need to adapt to the newer means while still following the old. For instance, on one hand you create a strong social media presence but, on the other hand, you don't stop publishing newspaper ads. Your strategy should be an innovative mix of traditional and post-modern. You have to reach all kinds of audiences. Since your goal is so high, you cannot afford to lose a single person. In such times, every single sold customer, every available prospect and even every single personal contact becomes a potentially valuable resource. These are the resources you need to rely on to reach potential customers.

When you reach your potential customers, you have to offer them something valuable that attracts them to choose your dealership. You cannot simply say, "We're the best dealership in town" even though you technically may be. That won't do. You need to offer the customers solid proof that you're capable of delivering on your promises. You have to attract potential customers with lucrative offers and attractive promotions. So, without wasting valuable time, let's get down to exploring the rationale of being everywhere.

When I entered the world of car sales, one of the areas I was most fascinated with were the various opportunities I had to reach and connect with potential clients. Not only was I becoming increasingly curious about the best ways to achieve that, I was falling more and more in love with the whole process.

I was introduced to the process by my Internet Director, with whom I'd spend hours at a time exploring our existing efforts to reach out to customers and create new ones. When other salespeople see me, they watch me interacting with customers, demonstrating vehicles, taking them on test drives and all the usual stuff. But what goes on behind the scenes is equally important. In fact, it's one of the key reasons for my success as a salesperson.

If you think car sales involves simply meeting people every day and showing them various vehicles only to pocket the commission at the end of the day, you're wrong. That is only one aspect of car sales— albeit a significant one. A point that many salespeople often ignore is that most of those customers don't just randomly enter the dealership one fine day. Their journey involved a long and complex behind-the-scenes process in which salespeople devised and followed strategies to drive walk-in traffic to the dealership. We work hard, and we spend a lot of time on the process. Even as we begin to yield the results and see a marked increase in walk-in traffic, we don't abandon it. Instead, we continue to increase our efforts.

To put it simply, if you want to increase your car sales numbers, you have to be everywhere. There is no other alternative and no easy way out. It is, quite simply, an unavoidable necessity. To put it in context, let's imagine a situation where you don't put in the effort to be everywhere. Let's say you are receiving fifty customers, on average, in a month, and you're closing approximately fifteen deals on a monthly basis. Where do you go from there? How do you ensure that more customers will walk in to your dealership? How can you double the amount of walk-in traffic?

Did you think of an alternative? The answer, of course, is no. No matter how attractive your offers are, no matter how good of a salesperson you are, no matter the quality of the products, if you don't actively strive to market those products and promotions, you're in a lot of trouble.

The only logical solution is to increase your presence. The car sales landscape is transforming at a rapid pace, and it's not all about the digital revolution. It's about the change in people's attitude. Many local dealerships find themselves in the midst of this change. The definitions of community are changing. The reliance of people on vehicles is lessening. Even when they do want to buy a vehicle, customers have a whole online avenue to explore. It's admittedly a bit of a discomforting atmosphere to be in, but you must quickly acquaint yourself and then find ways to conquer the rapidly changing landscape.

13 Steps to Increase Your Visibility and Reach More Clients

ACCLIMATE YOURSELF WITH CHANGING LANDSCAPE

Your first step to increasing your presence among potential prospects should be learning more about the changing car sales landscape and knowing it well. If someone asks you about your target audiences or the current trends in car sales, you need to be instantly able to provide a detailed answer.

For this step, you need to widen your horizons. You need to think not as a lone salesperson but as an analyst surveying the wider car sales landscape. You need to be up to speed with changing buyer behavior and the customers' expectations even before they walk into your dealership. All this information will make up your data set and greatly help you in the next step.

CREATE A DEFINITIVE STRATEGY TO REACH MORE CUSTOMERS

Now that you have all the required data to create an informed and educated strategy, it's time to get organized. Since your goal is highly elusive and you have a limited number of resources, you need to be creative with the use of those resources. The best way to do that is to prepare a strategy.

Your strategy should consist of defined steps that will help you reach all of the audiences that you identified in the previous step. You can divide your strategy into phases—start small and reach higher and higher goals. In the first phase, you can lay the foundation for your expansion by connecting to your existing sold customers and starting to build referral streams. In the second phase, you need to contact prospects through a variety of means. In the third phase, you use various forms of media to reach wider audiences. By breaking down the huge task into smaller and more achievable ones, you make it easier to focus on each of the specifics of the process, one at a time.

IDENTIFY AUDIENCES AND FIND WAYS TO REACH THEM

Usually, the creation of strategy and identification of audiences go hand in hand. Once you know which people you're trying to reach, you can find effective ways of reaching each of them in unique ways. To do this, I've created what I call a sales pipeline. This means that I've organized all my potential customers into various categories. Again, when I set out to sell thirty cars, I aim to sell to five customers in each of these categories:

1. Walk-in
2. Internet
3. Social Media
4. Web leads
5. Chat
6. Phone ups
7. Service
8. Referrals
9. Prospecting
10. Power base
11. Unsold

Once you break down your audiences into smaller categories, it's easier to find specific ways to reach each of the groups. For instance, how you reach Internet audiences is completely different from how you reach customers through phone calls. The demographic makeup of each audience may be different. Their mindset certainly differs, and your approach to capturing that mindset will definitely need to be unique. This brings us to our next step.

SET YOURSELF APART FROM YOUR COMPETITION

For every mass marketing campaign, you need something to market. It can be anything—a marketable product, a lucrative offer or a unique service feature. Without something to market, there's no point in carrying out the campaign. In car sales, the scope of coming up with something unique can be even more limited. You cannot compete on products since similar dealerships are selling more or less the same vehicle. That leaves only two options to compete over: prices and services.

I don't advise dealerships to compete over price. It takes you down a road you cannot afford. That leaves services. You need to come up with unique offers and promotions that are enticing for customers. You need to offer something concrete: this is what you'll get when you visit our dealership. It cannot be something vague or abstract like good service or exceptional treatment. Once you have something to market to your customers, you need to find the best ways to do it.

MAKE A SMART ADVERTISING CAMPAIGN THE CENTER OF YOUR PROMOTIONAL ACTIVITIES

This is where you get to flex your creative muscles. It's when you bring out the big guns. A well-thought-out and thought-provoking advertising campaign is the centerpiece of your strategy to expand your overall reach. It's one of the key ways you can attract more walk-in customers to your dealership, and you need to put all your creative input into making a smart advertising campaign to reach your customers.

But how exactly can you do that? It's obviously easier said than done. The first thing you need to do is observe what other dealerships are doing with their campaigns and, more importantly, where they are lacking. You then find ways to set yourself apart from the competition, and find the best ways to market your efforts.

USE A COMBINATION OF MEDIA OUTLETS

It's one thing to reach each potential prospect individually, and nothing beats personal contact. But that's not an alternative to reaching wider audiences. Think about that. With a well-placed, targeted media campaign, you can reach 100 in the same time it takes to reach only one person. Granted, this approach involves impersonal contact, and you cannot speak to each and every prospect individually. However, you make up for it by reaching various prospects at once.

Which media outlet is the best choice? There are many answers to this question, and none of them is the right one. Each medium is well-suited for its own purposes and reaches different audiences. There is also a significant overlap between mediums. Those who watch TV and use social media may hear your message twice on different channels, but that lends to your credibility and makes your message even more impactful.

Facebook is the most important of all the social media channels. It will, therefore, be the center of attention for a great part of your social media activity. However, you should not ignore some of the other important channels like Twitter, LinkedIn and Instagram. Sort all social media channels according to their user base, and assign different levels of priority to different social media channels.

CREATE A SOCIAL MEDIA STRATEGY

Whether you are operating on an individual basis as a lone salesperson or working on behalf of the whole organization, you need a social media strategy. Social media is the gateway to increasing your influence and being everywhere. More than 90 percent of your target audience is on social media, and a wide majority of those users spend an hour of their day, possibly more, browsing through the various social media channels. This is your playground; it's where you need to spend a lot of your advertising resources.

The first thing you need to do, when it comes to social media, is have a strong social media presence. And not only during office hours. You need to spend a considerable amount of your personal time building and cultivating a network of well-connected friends. Meeting new people is always fun. It's not tedious or boring in any way, so here's one area where you can have fun while getting closer to your objectives.

You're not doing this for fun and games, however. You're doing it to expand your social media influence. Personal influence is one of the key factors involved in increasing your social media reach. Your core group of friends and acquaintances are a gateway to a peripheral network of contacts. The larger the core, the bigger the periphery.

CREATE A WEBSITE

This is another step with equal scope of application on individual and institutional use. For instance, you can create a website for your dealership as well as your own personal website or a blog. The focus, here, is finding ways to make content interactive and build value for customers.

A blog is the ideal way to build value for customers. Creating informational or engaging content for potential prospects is a great way to give to the customers even before asking for something in return. Your website or blog can also serve as your personal lead generator. Potential prospects who contact you through your website are among the most valuable leads—and ones you won't find anywhere else. You should be the number one resource for any person who is looking to buy a car.

GENERATE GREAT CONTENT

We keep coming back to this point because it's the most important when it comes to expanding your presence among potential clients. If you are approaching a prospect, you must do so with something concrete to offer. Your prospect's time is valuable, and he won't waste it listening to what you have to say if you have nothing concrete to offer. Even if he does, he won't take away anything from it. So, each and every contact you make with your prospect, whether individually or through an advertising campaign, should be designed to provide value to him in one form or another.

This is why, when you set out to conquer the car sales market, you must generate great content. Your content is what provides value and attracts clients toward your message. Ultimately, the content is what the potential clients take away from the contact. Think about it—how many ads have you seen, heard or read in your life? The number must be in the tens if not hundreds of thousands. How many do you remember? Not many, I bet. Now think about why you remember the few that you do remember? You remember the ads that had something unique to offer. They were entertaining, engaging or informative in some way. You likely don't remember any of the more generic messages.

Your content is what makes your advertising campaign worthwhile. Whether you're trying to reach out to your clients through social media, your website or blog, a television ad campaign or even a telephone conversation, you must have something concrete to offer. Without it, you cannot sustain any advertising campaign because you cannot compel your prospects to remember the message, no matter how colorfully you present it. If you want to be everywhere, you need to understand the importance of creating great content.

However, this leads us to an important question. What should your ideal content look like? Which types of content should you focus on? The answer depends upon the type of audience you're trying to reach and, more importantly, the medium through which you're trying to reach them. For instance, radio and television are polar opposites. You cannot use similar content with both mediums. You cannot play the audio track from a TV ad for radio audiences. Your messages for TV and radio should be separately created with separate audiences in mind. With a TV ad, you can use visual and stylistic elements that would be of no use for radio.

Social media is where you can have most fun and variety with your content. Here again, the diverse nature of different channels matters. For instance, if you use Instagram to reach audiences, you need eye-catching images that make your dealership look like an attractive place to visit. You can photograph promotional activities and show others how those who visited had a lot of fun. As soon as you switch social media channels, however, the nature of your content changes accordingly. On Twitter, you have to create short but well-written messages. Whatever you say, you need to say it in fewer than 140 characters.

Facebook is the medium that allows for the most freedom in terms of the kinds of content you can push. The goal is to make it as engaging as possible. The more people who engage with your content, the higher it goes on the Facebook rankings and, in turn, the higher the number of people who see it on their home page. So, for instance, a new promotional announcement may not get as many likes, shares and comments as a Facebook contest to win discounts or other attractive gifts.

CREATE ATTRACTIVE PROMOTIONAL OFFERS

Never underestimate the value of a well-designed, well-thought-out promotional deal. Such an offer is not just another trick in your bag of tricks—it's one of the essential steps you need to take if you're planning to be everywhere. If you don't have a promotional deal, what do you have to offer potential clients? You can't exactly market the products themselves because every one of your competitors has more or less the same products to offer. You cannot artificially lower prices because, well, you can't afford to. And, even if you could in the short term, that's not a sustainable approach. The only things you're left with are periodic promotional offers that give you an excuse to reach out to people.

Let's make it simple. If you want to be everywhere, you *need* to have promotional offers. They are at the heart of all the activities you can carry out to attract customers. Not only do you need those attractive promotions, you also need to find ways to market those promotions. These two steps go hand in hand. If you are doing both of them well, you have a recipe for success.

One of the biggest challenges you can encounter in this area is a lack of ideas. It's easy to run out of things to offer. You cannot continue to offer only discounts every time; that gets too monotonous. Here are some ideas to consider for your next promotional offer. Alternate back and forth between these ideas to keep it fresh.

Sponsorships

One of the easiest ways to spend money and get your dealership's name across with minimal effort is to sponsor local teams. All you do is hand over payment and merchandise to those teams, sit back and enjoy the game.

Express Saturdays

If you have even the slightest experience working in a car dealership, you know that weekends are among the busiest days. Since people are busy with work during the week, most choose weekends for shopping for vehicles. This gives you a chance to make the most out of the opportunity. You can create express Saturday deals wherein you offer discounts and special maintenance deals for customers who cannot make it to the dealership on weekdays.

Games

When we talk about offering value to the customers, it's not always about trying to cram their heads full of unwanted information. Sometimes it works best to simply offer them opportunities to have a bit of fun. And what better "fun" opportunity can you offer than games? Offering discounts in return for fun activities is a win-win for the client while also being good for your business. Not only do the customers have a great time, they also get a discount or gift out of it. You can organize these games on the dealership floor and even on social media to engage more audiences.

Customer Rewards

You likely know how important I believe it is to generate repeat clients. Although each individual customer contributes to your business in a substantial way, repeat clients are your permanent resource. And, to encourage customer loyalty, you need to create offers to reward loyalty. Why should your customers step into your dealership again? What's in it for them? You can offer all sorts of things from discounts and complementary offers to movie tickets and free dinners.

USE YOUR CUSTOMER DATABASE TO EXPAND YOUR REACH

Your customer database is an ever-reliable resource. Whether following up with sold customers or contacting prospects, you need a well-maintained and well-organized database. There are many other uses for such a database as well, and one of those is to expand your reach among customers and prospects.

Simply put, when you have a customer database, you already have a well-established network of contacts. These are contacts you have personally dealt with, who know you as well; it's not a group of random people. It's a network of people who know and trust one another to a certain degree. You have their trust, and you need their contacts. You can easily expand your network by tapping into the personal contact base of each and every individual customer. Additionally, there's also the unexplored territory of the potential buyers. The opportunities are truly endless.

My own personal database, *The Autominer*, allows me to do all this and more. But that's not the only reason it's so reliable when it comes to expanding my or the dealership's reach. It does more than simply allow me to explore new networks or learn more about existing ones. It offers me an organized platform through which I can contact clients with minimal effort. The organization of information is the key; it saves time and is incredibly efficient.

OFFER TEST-DRIVING INCENTIVES

Many people simply don't understand that it doesn't matter whether or not you gave a mind-blowing presentation. It doesn't matter whether or not you used an ingenious advertising campaign. It doesn't matter whether or not you offer premium customer service. Some people are simply hard to please. On the other hand, there are people who just don't believe anything you have to say. They value their own experience a lot more than yours. They don't believe anything unless they've tried it themselves. For those kinds of people, there's a wonderful solution. It's called a test drive.

The challenge is that not all of those hard-to-please customers are willing to come to your dealership. They wonder why they should make an effort. After all, they don't need to drive over to a place just to drive another vehicle. But, everyone likes to go to a movie with his family or have dinner in an expensive restaurant, so why not combine all these activities? Why not offer the customer an opportunity to win those tickets or that dinner in return for a test drive? They have nothing to lose now. They're getting a free test drive and a chance to win discounts or gifts. This type of offer will attract even the most difficult customers.

Offering test-drive initiatives is not only a great way to attract customers, it's also one of the reasons to get in touch with more prospects. It gives you a reason to advertise. It gives you that concrete "thing," that value-building opportunity around which you can build an advertising campaign. If you're creative, you won't let this opportunity go.

BUILD STEADY REFERRAL STREAMS

If your goal is to be everywhere, you can't rely solely on mass media. Although advertising is a great way to get your message out there, it has its limitations. One of those limitations is the impersonality that comes with it. You lose the personal touch, the opportunity for a conversation. The only medium that, however remotely, allows the opportunity to converse, is social media, but even that remote possibility is lost in other mediums such as TV or Radio.

This is why you need to go old school. You need to pick up that phone and start calling people. There's simply no alternative to a genuine, human one-to-one conversation. You're already doing that through the follow-up, so you may be wondering how it's different in this scenario. Here your goal is to gain as many referrals as possible. In fact, your goal is to create a steady referral stream whereby customers continue to pour in on a regular basis.

One of the advantages of going after referrals is that, reaching people through a referral is much different from reaching them through social media. On social media, you're nobody. Why should a potential customer trust you? He has no prior experience with your services, nor does he know anyone who has interacted with you.

When you reach people through a referral, however, there is an element of trust, a sense of familiarity. They know you, or they at least know people who do. They know from people they trust that your products and services are great. When you reach them, it's different. Referrals are essential for your strategy; not only do they bring you into contact with new people, they also create more chances for a meaningful conversation.

Don't Give Up

* * *

"Never give up on something that you can't go a day without thinking about."
—Winston Churchill

One of the keys to success in car sales is passion. You need to have a burning desire to succeed in reaching your goals. When you have that passion, that sense of energy, you can never afford to give up. The only thing you can—and should—do is carry on toward the pursuit of your objectives. It doesn't matter if you stumble or fall. You need to get back on your feet again. Getting sidetracked comes with the job. All salespeople experience failure, but only the best of us have the ability to get back up on our feet.

When you set out to sell thirty cars per month, your chances for success depend upon two factors: ability and attitude. If you don't have the ability, it should go without saying that you don't stand much chance of being successful. But having the ability is not all you need to succeed. You also need to have the right attitude. Your attitude enables you to approach your problems with positivity and consider your failures to be nothing more than constructive learning experiences.

The only thing that can cause you to resist or refuse giving up is your approach to dealing with setbacks. When you set out on the journey to achieve your goals and dreams in sales, you will fail at times, as we all do. You will make mistakes, as we all do. Your ability to deal with those mistakes will define you as a salesperson. Some of the best salespeople welcome mistakes. They consider them a learning experience. They welcome them as opportunities to learn more about what they *shouldn't* do. This is the approach that paves the path toward success.

DEVELOP A WINNING ATTITUDE

It is great to be aware of the thought process behind a winning attitude. However, what's even more important is developing the ability to deal with specific problems that arise in the course of your pursuit of your goals. This advice is based on some of the challenges I experienced as a salesperson and what I did to overcome them.

BE PREPARED TO WORK HARD

When I entered the field of car sales, I was not remotely interested in pursuing it as a career. I even remember being offended when someone told me I looked like a car salesman. However, as I gradually explored more and more about car sales as a career, I fell more and more in love with it. Beyond that, I was competitive. I set goals for myself and wanted to achieve them in order to pursue a higher set of goals. I had a consistent drive to push the boundaries of what I could achieve further and further still.

When I look back and think about what enabled me to achieve such a spectacular level of success in this profession, one reason rises above all others: hard work. I succeeded because I worked hard toward the pursuit of my goals. I was prepared to give it my best shot, give it everything I had, and that's what I did. When you set out to achieve a difficult set of goals, always be prepared to give to the profession more—much more—than what's expected of you. Through hard work and dedication, you can solve any problem that comes your way.

SET REALISTIC GOALS FOR YOURSELF

This is one of the most important requirements for a winning attitude, and one that people often ignore. Many times, in their enthusiasm to go out and achieve their dreams, people bite off more than they can chew. Setting goals for yourself is the easy part. Anyone can set goals for himself. Pursuing those goals, however, is more difficult.

The reason that many of us give up is not the lack of talent or sound professional advice. It's the fact that, sometimes, our destination seems so far away that no matter what we do, it seems impossible that we'll ever reach it. When you set unrealistic goals for yourself, all you have is the illusion of progress. Even if you perform better than everyone else, you'll feel unaccomplished.

An example of a realistic goal in car sales is to sell thirty cars per month. It's a specific number that you strive to achieve. It's easily quantifiable. Some may believe that selling thirty cars in a month is a difficult task, and I would agree. But, setting realistic goals is not the same as setting *easy* goals. If you break down the 30-car target, you have to sell one to two cars per day, and that's manageable, even if it's a bit difficult. On the other hand, if your goal is to become the world's best salesperson in a matter of months or even years, that's unlikely to happen without a solid plan.

DON'T LET MISTAKES DISCOURAGE YOU

Let's face it, everyone makes mistakes. Even the most experienced and successful salespeople make mistakes. In that respect, all salespeople are alike. However, those with a winning approach to the pursuit of their goals don't let their mistakes get in the way of success. On the other hand, little failures are one of the biggest reasons many younger salespeople never take off and give up so easily.

Being a professional car salesperson means that we have to do what we do on a daily basis. We have to deal with all kinds of customers. Some are easy to work with while others are not. No two sales are alike. The circumstances of each sales opportunity differ widely. The nature of the customers, their willingness to buy and the quality of your customer service are just a few of the factors that feed into a sales equation. While, sometimes, everything fits together in spectacular fashion, there are times where none of the individual elements come together. That's when you need to realize that this is just one opportunity in a series of many. Of course, each customer is valuable and you should do everything in your power to prevent losing him. But, sometimes, you must let go of some of your mistakes in order to start anew the next day and make sure you don't repeat the mistake.

DEFINE THE PROBLEMS AND TAKE A SYSTEMATIC APPROACH TOWARD A SOLUTION

The path to every sales goal can be littered with innumerable small and large problems. Your job is to navigate that path while trying to carefully avoid those problems.

Sometimes, however, you're unable to do that, and the only available option is to face your problem head-on.

It sounds easy enough in theory, but in practice it can be challenging to identify the problem, let alone face it. If you ask salespeople the reason for their poor numbers, many of them won't be able to identify a single reason or a set of reasons. Your goal is to take your performance to even greater heights, and that's not possible without rectifying potential problems.

The first step is to correctly define the problem. To do that, you need sharp observation, a degree of introspection and feedback from your customers. When you have all the data, it's easy to identify the gaps and spot where the problem lies. Once you're able to reach the core of the issue, you need to form a strategy to resolve it. An organized series of steps not only makes the path ahead clearer, it also provides you with a set of achievable smaller goals that combine to form one larger goal.

SEEK INSPIRATION FROM YOUR COMPETITION

If you want to succeed in car sales, you need to surround yourself with the right people. These are the people who are the high-achievers in your profession. They are the ones who set a standard for others. They may be your competition in sales terms, but they are an example as well. They have years of experience on their side. Try to benefit from their experience and learn from their mistakes. Never hesitate to reach out to them for guidance. Observe their actions. From the tiniest hand gestures to their more overt body language, from the way they greet the customers to the way they negotiate, everything they do can provide a learning opportunity.

Your competition can offer many opportunities for inspiration, but some salespeople are easily intimidated. Those of you who get discouraged—rather than inspired by—high-flyers need to readjust your perspective. Even though you may be engaged in some sort of competitive endeavor with some of the most experienced colleagues, your job is not to compete with them; it's to compete with yourself. You need to continue to improve, month after month. You need to benchmark your performance against yourself. How many more cars are you selling this month compared to the previous ones? How many more customers are you dealing with, and how many more deals are you closing? These are the questions you need to keep asking yourself.

The most important consideration when it comes to working in a competitive environment is, the best salespeople in the industry once started as rookies. They were once in the same situation as you. They made the same mistakes you do, and they went through the same process you're going through. The only difference is that they never gave up.

Afterword

* * *

When I entered the car sales industry, I had no definitive sense of direction. Even though I had mentors like Jim DiMeo who guided me every step of the way, my growth was organic. I had to make my own way in an increasingly competitive and difficult environment. I had to fall, get up and fall again. I had to make mistakes, learn from them and make new ones. It was an extremely harsh journey, and it was up to me to discover what worked and what didn't. This book is a collection of all the little discoveries I made and the knowledge that was passed on to me by my seniors.

I never set out to be a manager. I set out to be the number one salesperson and receive a respectable paycheck in order to feed my family. I never realized I could make $20,000-$25,000 a month selling cars. I am proof that you don't have to be the greatest salesperson in the world, you only have to be willing to learn and apply yourself. It is true that knowledge is power. But what good is knowledge without action or the willingness to apply it?

I now help run one of the Top 10 Toyota dealerships in the nation. If it weren't for my efforts to learn and apply what I've learned from the people around me as well as my mentor, I wouldn't be where I am today. Even though I am one of the top earners in my field, I'm not finished, and I will continue to learn and apply what I've learned.

CHARLES MAUND TOYOTA

The journey to Charles Maund Toyota's success was not easy. However, with a fixed set of rules, support from the staff and tons of hard work, we were able to take our dealership through uncharted territories into the land of success. With car sales exceeding 1000 per month, we are the #1 dealership in Austin, Texas and on our way to being one of the best in the country. We have some of the best sales staff working around the clock to manage walk-in customers, follow up with existing clients and contact leads to secure new customers. Everything functions like a well-oiled machine, and we continue to climb higher in the hierarchy of top American dealerships.

But all this success didn't happen overnight. It was a product of hard work and teamwork. We put in weeks, months, even years of hard work to build the machinery that functions so effortlessly today. We worked hard on every single potential customer to turn him into a repeat client. We put a great deal of thought into our sales process and how we implement our business strategy in a way that's mutually beneficial for us and for our customers. We continue to fine-tune our process to perfection. A twist here and a tweak there, it took collective effort to reach where we are today.

Every day we tried, and every day we failed to a degree. We made a lot of mistakes, but we never repeated the same mistake. It was our experience that became our salvation, our willpower that became our energy, and we were able to harness the power of the two elements to pave a way where there was none. We cemented our position in the marketplace, expanded outward and are continuing to do so to this very day. The journey was fraught with complexities and seemingly impossible targets that we not only achieved but surpassed.

When we first started out on our journey, we were able to double our current performance in the first month of sales. The store was selling 150 cars per month and we reached the 350 mark within the first few months. For any other dealership, that might have been enough. Many stores around the country would be happy selling 350 cars per month. We could have stopped there, and the company would have been profitable for many years. But we decided not to go down that path. Complacency is the enemy of success. If you are content with whatever meager achievements you have to date, you should stop dreaming about a better future right now.

This is precisely why there's such a huge disparity between the national car sales numbers and the sales performance of individual dealerships. Complacency is the key determining factor. It may come as a surprise to you, but most of the car sales franchise stores across the country average 150 new and fifty used car sales per month. You may be more shocked to learn that many of these stores seem to be happy with their performance. How can you rise up to capture the emerging market if it's not a priority for you? How can you sell 1000 cars per month if you don't even want to?

Some people call it financial complacency. The problem is not that you don't have the right abilities, it's that you don't have the right mindset to make full use of those abilities. You need to keep growing in order to secure a definitive place in the community. You also need to dominate the marketplace like no one has before. The only way to achieve that is to avoid stagnation and complacency. You have to push yourself, will yourself, drive yourself and even drag yourself if necessary. The only way to go is on. And the only thing to do is work hard, and give it your best.

This is what we did at Charles Maund Toyota. We were willing to do anything and everything to reach the level we wanted and then go beyond it. It was a challenge to perform with the same amount of energy day-in and day-out over weeks, months and years. But we had inspiration. We were inspired by the best, and even the worst, examples.

The best included Longo Toyota in California, which is the number one Toyota dealership on the planet and has continued to be for almost fifty years. Longo sells approximately 1800 new cars and 500 used cars per month. That inspires us to continuously raise our standards despite the enormous success we've had over the years.

We were also inspired by the lowest of the low, the dealerships that sell only 20-60 cars per month. We were inspired *not* to be like them. I, for one, cannot bear to think about how some dealerships can continue to be so complacent at selling cars when there's a treasure trove of knowledge and experience all around them. Admittedly, finding all that knowledge in one place can be difficult, but that's why I was inspired to write this book. If you are facing challenges increasing your sales numbers, try to do what we did, which has been detailed throughout this book.

I intended to design this book to deconstruct the sales process and examine each and every aspect of it. Through that process of discovery, we can gain insight into some of the best sales practices available to help us achieve our goals. Whether you are starting out in the car sales arena, attempting to boost your sales performance or simply looking to earn money in this industry, this book can act as a comprehensive guide to achieving the goal of selling thirty cars per month.

The information in this book won't make you a successful salesperson overnight; it only lays the path ahead. If you want to travel down that path, you need absolute commitment to the pursuit of your goals. Skill and talent can take you only so far. You need perseverance and dedication as well. I am not the best salesperson in the world, but what I do have is absolute dedication to the achievement of my goals. That's how I develop the focus required to improve my sales performance.

I did not reach my goal of selling thirty cars per month overnight. It took a lot of hard work to reach that point. This book is only a guide for the complex and challenging—yet extremely rewarding—journey of car sales, but you have to travel down that path yourself.

I wish you the best of luck in that endeavor!

To inquire about speaking opportunities or other bookings as well as learn more about the latest sales strategies we are employing to sell more and more cars each month, please visit my website at: http://www.ChrisJosephMartinez.com.

Made in the USA
Lexington, KY
17 May 2017